SOUTHERN COUNTRY STATIONS: 2

SOUTH EASTERN & CHATHAM RAILWAY

SOUTHERN COUNTRY STATIONS: 2
SOUTH EASTERN & CHATHAM RAILWAY

JOHN MINNIS

LONDON

IAN ALLAN LTD

STATION
SHEPHERDSWELL NEAR DO

First published 1985

ISBN 0 7110 1500 7

Published by Ian Allan Ltd, Shepperton, Surrey;
and printed by Ian Allan Printing Ltd at their works
at Coombelands in Runnymede, England

**Unless otherwise indicated all photographs
are by the author.**

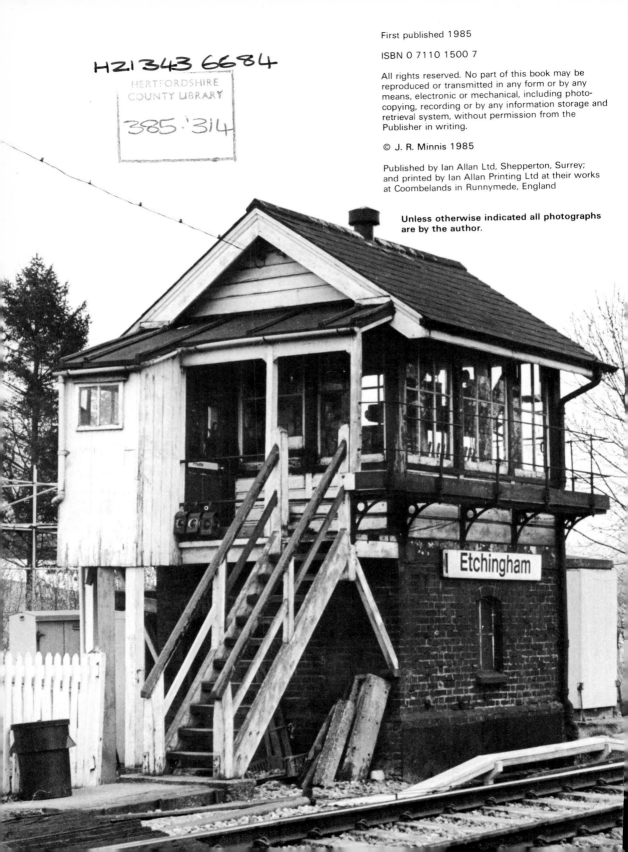

Contents

Preface

Bexley Libraries for their photographic assistance. To the Chief Civil Engineer, British Rail Southern Region and his staff for their help. To D. Clayton for the loan of negatives and to the other photographers named in the text. Finally, I owe a great debt to the draftsmanship of William Rowley who has produced the majority of the drawings and to Kate Rowley for all her help throughout the writing of this book.

John Minnis
Brighton

My aim, in writing this book, has been to provide an introduction to the country stations of what has until recently been a very neglected railway. My interpretation of the word 'country' has been flexible and I have included a number of stations now well within the clutches of suburbia which were for many years surrounded mainly by fields. I have also included a number of stations that are quite well known but which had to be covered on account of their architectural quality. I make no claim for the present work to be, in any sense, the definitive history of the SECR's architecture, merely an introduction to certain aspects of it. Unlike the Great Western Railway, covered by Chris Leigh in the first volume in this series, a large proportion of the buildings still exist and I have had an interesting time visiting and photographing those that are left.

I have had a great deal of help from many people in producing this book and I would like to give my thanks to the following. To my fellow members of the South Eastern & Chatham Railway Society, especially Tony Riley, Malcolm Parker and Chris Perkins who has produced some superb drawings. To P. Kay for letting me see the manuscript of his forthcoming work on signalboxes. To John Smith of Lens of Sutton and

A note on the drawings

The majority are based on original contract drawings and consequently, one cannot guarantee that every detail of the buildings eventually constructed conformed to them. However, most tally closely with photographic evidence. Where there are subsequent changes, these are noted by the individual drawings. Some drawings are based mainly on photographs; again, they may not be accurate in every dimension but I do not think they fall far short.

Below:
Set in the beautiful rolling hills of the High Weald, Cranbrook is seen here on 22 July 1933. A fine composition, it represents the station as a homeward bound rambler might have stumbled upon it. The cast iron notice headed South Eastern & Chatham Railway Companies Managing Committee reminds us that we are talking about two companies when we use the expression SECR. The station is little altered from the day it opened in 1893. The large goods warehouse with its sliding end door is just visible. *H. C. Casserley*

6

Introduction

The South Eastern & Chatham Railway has never had a very good press. The two partners in the working union were the subject of derision, sometimes justly, sometimes undeserved. The rolling stock was, of course, notorious. Ahrons's jibes of trains giving 'the impression of moving castellated walls' are certainly borne out when one examines photographs. How far did stations coincide with this popular image of greedy companies exploiting the passenger for all he was worth and ploughing back the minimum amount of capital for his comfort? There is no single answer to this question; it depends very much on the period and lines referred to. Both railways were very much lines of contrast where a superb piece of architecture might be located next to an undistinguished wooden shed.

I use the expression both railways because, in fact, there was no such thing as an SECR country station: there were SER stations and LCDR stations. It is often forgotten that the 1899 working agreement was just that, an agreement and not a merger, and that while the Chief Mechanical Engineer's department was eventually united under Wainwright at Ashford, no such unity ever applied to the practices of the Chief Civil Engineer's department. Both railways retained their own distinctive architectural traditions and, in

any case, nearly all the rural stations were built prior to 1899.

For a contemporary view of the standard of facilities provided at stations we can do no better than turn to J. Pearson Pattinson who anonymously wrote three small books between 1895 and 1897 about the LBSCR, the LCDR and the SER. While much space was devoted to analysis of train performance, these volumes were in effect consumers guides to the railways – rather as if *Which* magazine were to carry out such a survey today.

Pearson Pattinson was not particularly impressed with the South Eastern:

'Station accommodation varies greatly. Sometimes good, sometimes bad, more frequently indifferent, the general standard cannot rank very high.'

'Most of the smaller stations on the main line are somewhat heavy-looking wooden structures, and often these, although giving fair accommodation, have been allowed to go without paint for a very considerable time, with manifest injury to the appearance of the wood-work. The colour used is a dull white, which might with advantage be relieved and heightened by the judicious employment of one or two other tints. On the other hand, at several small stations – and these, singularly enough, generally on branch lines –

Below:
As with other railways in the Edwardian era, the SECR provided a number of halts. These were of plain but neat design. Leigh Halt, between Tonbridge and Penshurst, was opened in 1911. One of the early 'A' class 4-4-0s designed by Stirling draws in. *Lens of Sutton*

Above:
Blackwater and Wokingham had brick stations of Tudor design. The diapered brickwork stands out clearly on the gable in this view of Blackwater c1900. The platforms are still very low and the level crossing gates are of the early vertical timbered type. *A. M. Riley collection*

neglect of this sort was not conspicuous. Among these may be mentioned Gomshall, Chilworth and Shalford on the Reading line; Nutfield, near Redhill; Ticehurst Road and Battle, on the Hastings line; and one or two others. A pleasing feature is the decorating of stray stations here and there with flower beds and plants. Smeeth, Wadhurst and Sidcup are very noticeable examples. Overbridges and subways are for the most part provided to ensure safety in crossing the line.'

The London Chatham & Dover Railway can hardly be said to have fared any better:

'The station accommodation provided by the Chatham and Dover cannot be said to rank high. On the whole it would appear scarcely equal to that found on the South Eastern Railway, the standard of both companies being distinctly poor.'

'Journeying down the main line we find the roadside stations consist of a two storey brick building containing the stationmaster's residence, with a ground floor annexe serving as booking-office and waiting-room. A very short, low screen gives but indifferent protection from wind and weather and the accommodation generally may be summed up as merely passable.

'It is, however, on its coast and branch lines that the company possesses the best stations.'

'The smaller stations on the branches are only here and there deficient, and at certain points – Otford, Wrotham and Malling, for instance – there is ground for praise. The finest roadside stations on the system are to be found at Bearsted, Hollingbourne, Harrietsham, Lenham and Charing on the Maidstone and Ashford line. These tasteful modern structures have been generally carried out in dark red brick, and rank not far below the best branch line stations of the Brighton Railway in point of liberal roadside accommodation.'

'Floral decoration of station platforms is usual to a small extent, the best display on the line being made at Kearsney, near Dover . . .'

'The signalboxes, footbridges (ironwork), water tanks and sundry other appointments of the line would gain much in appearance if painted some uniform colour, or combination of colours, as is done on the London Brighton and South Coast.'

In contrast to most other parts of the country, it is still possible to write of SECR country stations in the present, rather than the past tense. There has been little in the way of closures and relatively few stations have been completely rebuilt in recent years. In particular, the LCDR line from Swanley to Ashford and the SER lines from Strood to Paddock Wood and Tonbridge to Hastings retain much of their pre-grouping flavour with nearly all the stations intact, together with signalboxes and ancillary structures. That all three lines pass through delightful countryside is an added bonus. It is perhaps a paradox that the Kentish lines were electrified relatively early before the process became one involving the installation of modern signalling and extensive trackwork revision and this has helped preserve them very much as they were in the 1950s.

The South Eastern Railway

The platform side at Rye, looking towards Hastings in June 1948. Behind the platform fence is the equally splendid goods warehouse, designed by Tress in 1851. *D. Clayton*

1 The Timber Station

The first stretch of the South Eastern Railway to open (with the notable exceptions of the Canterbury & Whitstable Railway and the London & Greenwich Railway) was the main line leaving the London & Brighton Railway at Redhill and running to Ashford. The platforms at the principal through stations at Tonbridge, Paddock Wood and Ashford were served by loops off the main lines, a highly progressive feature for 1842. All three were equipped with substantial brick buildings. The wayside stations with which we are concerned here were highly standardised and set the prevailing style for the SER until the end of its separate existence.

These stations, located at Godstone (rebuilt 1914), Edenbridge, Penshurst, Marden, Staplehurst, Headcorn and Pluckley, were all of the staggered platform arrangement. This layout, although utilised to some extent by many companies in their early days, became the trademark of the SER. The track configuration with its up and down sidings became even more standardised than the architecture. The idea behind staggered platforms was that alighting passengers would always cross the tracks behind the train from which they had disembarked and so were less likely to run the risk of being knocked down. In later years platform extensions have tended to disguise the practice but Wateringbury, Sturry and Ham Street are good surviving examples.

The chosen design for the earliest wayside stations was simple yet adequate for the traffic; three of the buildings are still used for the same purpose for which they were built 143 years ago. At a time when many companies chose to erect cottage-like structures reminiscent of the lodges to a great house or, in the case of the GWR, highly sophisticated small buildings, the South Eastern adopted the humble Kentish vernacular clapboard methods of construction. Other railways put up similar structures in the 1840s but they were generally intended to be purely temporary, to last until the upsurge in traffic warranted the erection of something more substantial. One example is Eastbourne, which the LBSCR built in 1849. From the 1860s onwards the needs of economy dictated the use of small timber buildings, often prefabricated, throughout much of the railway system. So in the long term the South Eastern's decision to build cheap stations was vindicated since the majority of other railway companies were eventually obliged to follow suit.

Each building was single storey with a shallow pitched roof of slate. The walls were of horizontal clapboarding. One noticeable difference between these buildings and the many that followed them was the total absence of shelter for passengers on the platform; canopies came much later, and of these early stations only Penshurst ever received one. Fenestration has changed over the years. Originally windows were either of the casement type or were sashes with the panes divided in the Georgian manner into the very pleasing arrangement of four panes per sash. Over the years, however, these have been replaced by the conventional Victorian two panes per sash. Because of the type of construction, changes in the position of window and door openings were easy to achieve. Other noticeable changes include the provision of guttering and the raising of platforms which makes the buildings look rather squat.

Godstone was replaced early, Edenbridge circa 1970, Penshurst in 1924 (it burnt down) and Staplehurst in the 1960s. Marden, Headcorn and Pluckley, remarkably, survive, though one wonders how much of the original fabric remains beyond the basic frame.

Other stations of the same basic design continued to be built over the next few years, for example at East Farleigh and Yalding in 1844 (the latter burnt down in 1893) and Chilham in 1846 (demolished circa 1970). The remaining stations on the Ashford–Canterbury line were substantial brick structures. No more wooden stations were to be built for nearly 20 years.

The next burst of timber building came in the 1860s, a time when other railway companies were turning to this form of construction. The first batch were those on the new line from Hither Green to Dartford, opened in 1866, being the stations of Lee, Mottingham, Sidcup, Bexley and Crayford. All were simple clapboarded structures, the one major advance being the use of awnings mounted on cast iron pillars to protect travellers from the elements. In contrast, an extraordinary building was erected at Earley circa 1863 which resembled nothing more than one of the timber stations set on top of a lower brick storey.

A further group of stations in a generally simpler style were those on the new direct main line to Tonbridge of 1868. Again the buildings were highly standardised. Those at Hildenborough, Dunton Green and Chelsfield were almost identical, while slightly larger examples of the same type were put up at Orpington and Sevenoaks. The precursor of the type was Chislehurst, opened in 1865. The same style was employed for the new stations opened on existing lines in the 1870s. Grove Park (1871) was virtually identical to the Hildenborough pattern while New Eltham (1878) and Knockholt (1876) were twins, being distinguished by the semicircular top to their platform awnings and a distinctive valancing pattern. The stations at Hythe and Sandgate were built to a similar design in 1874.

Bromley still retained much of the appearance of a

country town in 1878 when a branch was built from Grove Park to serve it. Both Bromley North and the intermediate station, Sundridge Park, were typical rural branch line stations. Sundridge Park had a small booking office at a higher level with the platforms in a cutting. The supports for the canopy over its entrance were simply formed of wooden struts rather than the decorative cast iron variety normally employed for this purpose. The terminus at Bromley was a longer building, again with wood canopy supports, and the most common type of valancing. The station's layout was curious, the three roads ending in a turntable. The station certainly gave the impression of being constructed 'on the cheap' with even the platform edged in timber. The sagging timbers of the rapidly decaying station building were flanked by sundry old carriage bodies and a motley collection of sheds. By the 1920s it was regarded as one of the worst stations on the system and the newly formed Southern Railway rebuilt it in 1925 as a matter of priority.

Brasted and Westerham stations, opened in 1881, were unique in that they had external metal brackets below the soffit and cast iron supports for the canopy on the road side. The awning was more highly pitched than usual and the windows were paired. The branch was built by the Westerham Valley Railway, a nominally independent concern, and the contract drawings for the station bear its name. Sharnal Street and Cliffe stations on the new line to Port Victoria were built to the same drawing in 1882. These had sashes with only one pane per sash and canopies mounted on wooden brackets. The same year Eden Park and Hayes stations were opened. They were of a similar type but larger and had windows with four panes per sash, most of the windows being paired.

In 1883/4 Tovil, a new station to serve a suburb of Maidstone, opened. It does not appear to have had a canopy. In contrast to the corrugated iron stations of the light railway pattern favoured at the other stations on the Elham Valley line, opened in 1881, those at Elham itself and Lyminge were of the timber pattern, and the same design was used for Ore in 1888. A notable variation on the theme occurred when Northfleet was rebuilt in 1891. The windows were paired in the way of several other stations of this pattern but the tops of the windows were rounded which gave the building a most distinctive appearance. Valancing was of the conventional type.

The last batch of timber stations to be constructed in a rural area were those on the Bexleyheath Loop line of 1895. This part of North Kent was very much open countryside when the line was built. Buildings at Kidbrooke, Eltham Well Hall, Welling, Bexleyheath and Barnehurst were of similar design, the only variation being at Barnehurst where the booking office was at right angles to the line and on a higher level. Smitham, opened in 1904, was the last example of all but, as the area in which it was situated was almost entirely built up by then, it is doubtful whether it should be considered as a rural station.

Right:
The same station on 3 June 1984 showing the effects of 108 years of change. The window and door openings have been altered, casements being replaced by sashes. The cladding is now composed of narrower clapboarding and corner posts have been added. The rafter ends have disappeared and the toilets have been moved to the other end of the building. The raising of the platform has had the effect of totally altering the proportions of the station; it now appears much lower than it did when built.

Centre right:
Another view of Pluckley from the forecourt, bringing out the neat effect of the clapboarding. Here too, no protection from the elements was provided.

Below right:
The next station towards London, Headcorn, displays many of the same characteristics as Pluckley. The photograph is a little later, probably c1880, and the station has undergone slightly more in the way of change. The cladding above the doors and windows has been altered, pointing to a possible change in their respective positions. A hipped roof signalbox has replaced the original hut. Goods facilities are provided in the shape of a small brick shed. Posing for the photographer are two men on one of those hand-powered cars beloved of the makers of Western movies.
Lens of Sutton

Below:
Comparison with the previous photograph shows just how much a timber building could be altered. Every window and door opening has been modified, windows being replaced by doorways and vice versa. Two of the original type of casements are still in place and are joined by two different patterns of sash, all within the same elevation. The gentlemen's toilet has been rebuilt at the opposite end of the building from its former position and the roof has been clad in asbestos. Photographed 3 June 1984.

Top:
**Staplehurst is of similar design but this photograph
taken on 31 October 1887 gives a good idea of the
traffic in a country goods yard. Packaging is in the form
of sacks and wicker baskets while most of the wagons
visible are SER standard opens with high round ends,
although a variation with cut away ends can be seen
behind. Although the station was rebuilt in the 1960s,
the gabled warehouses are still in existence and are
pictured in Chapter 14.** *Lens of Sutton*

Right:
**Marden, here photographed in June 1984, has had
fewer changes to the fabric of the building than
Headcorn or Pluckley. It retains the wide tongue and
groove boarding and casement windows, although it has
been re-roofed in corrugated asbestos and has lost its
chimneys.**

Above:
**The road side of Marden reveals more change. A canopy
has been fitted over the booking hall entrance and the
casement windows replaced by sashes. The rather
curious piece of wall to the left is all that remains of the
goods warehouse.**

Top:
A smaller version of the design, Penshurst, looking towards Tonbridge in 1870. The distinctive SER track layout and platform arrangements should now be clear. The station buildings on this stretch of line have sash windows as opposed to casements, while additional sheds have sprung up. The goods shed is a little larger than that at Headcorn and has a goods office at the rear, added in 1864. An end loading dock occupied by a horsebox stands at the end of the up siding. The signal is of the early double slotted type: the use of a white dot instead of a vertical band was a unique SER practice that lasted until the grouping. *Lens of Sutton*

Above:
The same scene at Penshurst, c1905, providing a fascinating comparison with the accompanying photograph. Although the basic structures remain, all the details have changed completely. The station building has been fitted with a canopy bearing the familiar SER valancing which has transformed its appearance, as has the raising of platform levels. Iron platform fencing has replaced wooden post and rail, a station nameboard of standard SECR design has been added and, as was generally the case, the early signal hut just visible beyond the canopy has been turned into a store, superseded by the handsome and commodious Railway Signal Co box of 1893 opposite. The track layout remains unaltered. Following a severe fire, the station building was replaced in 1924 by a rather attractive neo-Tudor design designed to harmonise with the picturesque village nearby. This went the way of most station buildings on the Tonbridge–Reading line in 1970. *Lens of Sutton*

Below:
A Fairburn Class 4 2-6-4T draws the 9.42 Ashford–Margate stopping train into Chilham on 8 April 1953. The 1846 station building lasted in its original form until demolition c1970. The plain three bay goods warehouse of 1861, with its recessed panels, slightly resembles contemporary LBSC designs. The signalbox, an example of the Saxby & Farmer style with deep overhanging eaves and dating from 1893, was later removed to Tenterden Town on the preserved Kent & East Sussex Railway where it was re-erected.
Donald Kelk

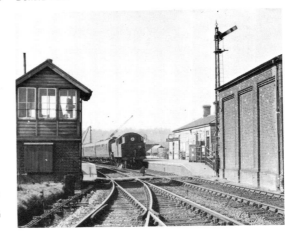

Above:
Certainly the oddest variation on the theme of timber stations was at Earley where a standard timber superstructure was erected on top of a narrow brick base. This gave it the look of being suspended in mid air. Shaped wooden brackets were used to support the upper storey of the building which dated from 1863. Beside it is one of the ubiquitous 'roader' sheds while beyond is the signalbox, a typical hipped roof example, painted up with a dark base and light upper works in the usual SER style. The station nameboard still retains (c1905) the painted lettering with shading. This type of board seems to have been in use from the earliest days to the turn of the century. *Lens of Sutton*

Below:
Knockholt, then known as Halstead, looking southwards c1880. The station, which was opened in 1876, displays the progress made since the first timber stations of 30 years earlier: platforms are no longer staggered and are higher, and the buildings are now fitted with canopies. That on the down platform was clearly intended to match the principal building on the up side, giving the station a unified appearance. An all wood footbridge was provided for crossing the main line (Pluckley did not acquire one until the 1950s). Close boarding remained in vogue for platform fencing until the end of the century as did the delightful 'Gentlemen' sign which was, with its shading and scrollwork, a standard SER fitting. *Lens of Sutton*

Left:
The road side of Knockholt, photographed in 1976, with the station virtually unaltered. An unusual feature was the letter box set in a brick surround. The building has subsequently been demolished.

Below:
East Farleigh is a delightful spot. It lies in a typical Kentish setting with oast houses and hopfields on the east bank of the River Medway, which flows under the 14th century bridge past a timber framed farmhouse. The station is appropriately in the best SER vernacular style with matching signalbox. The core of the building is the original structure of 1844, similar that to destroyed by fire at Yalding in 1893, although the windows have been altered and the accommodation increased. The other platform is located out of the picture beyond the level crossing. This photograph was taken on 19 April 1981.

Left:
The old station at Bromley North was an extraordinary affair. When the station was opened in 1878, Bromley was already a substantial town with considerable commuter traffic on the LCDR line. Despite this the SER station looked more akin to one on a light railway. The platforms were faced with wood, all the buildings were wooden and supplementary accommodation was provided by an old carriage body. The passenger roads led to a turntable, shown in this photograph of July 1921, together with the engine house which has attracted a fair quantity of vegetation. The station building itself is obscured by the tree on the left. That this photograph was taken in a major suburb 10 miles from Charing Cross seems scarcely credible. It is little wonder the Southern Railway promptly rebuilt the place in 1925. *H. J. Patterson Rutherford*

Left:
Sharnal Street on the branch to Port Victoria on 5 June 1928 before a second platform was added. Built in 1882, the building is very similar in appearance to that at Knockholt. Again, note the timber edge to the platform. The signalling at this simple station in the remote and bleak Hundred of Hoo is still of the SER pattern. *H. A. Vallance*

Below:
Westerham, a perfect country branch terminus, has received much attention over the years and deservedly so. It is the ideal size for modellers, having all the basic facilities with a compact track layout. In this 1965 photograph several points call for examination. The Stevens signalbox is of a type usually associated with the LCDR, and the goods warehouse is a particularly attractive timber structure. *C. J. Perkins*

Bottom:
The platform elevation of Westerham station in 1965. *C. J. Perkins*

WESTERHAM VALLEY RAILWAY
STATION BUILDING

RAIL LEVEL

ELEVATION (FROM RAILS)

ELEVATION (FROM APPROACH)

SCALE OF FEET

10   5   0   10   20   30

Above:
Westerham station building. The drawing depicts the structure as built. It was subsequently extended slightly at the Dunton Green end as shown in the photographs.
Drawing by W. E. Rowley

Right:
Boxhill is on an embankment, hence the narrow, wooden platforms in this view of c1910 looking towards Betchworth, with the slopes of Boxhill itself visible in the background. A great many wooden brackets seem to have been deemed necessary to support the canopy on the left. The signalbox is a rare all wood variety of the Saxby & Farmer pattern. *Lens of Sutton*

Far right:
Bexleyheath, opened in 1895, represents the final development of the timber design. It is, in most respects, identical to its predecessors of the 1860s. The waiting shelters on this line were distinctive in having the roofs dropping down to the rear in a gentle curve. Here a Stirling 'Q' class 0-4-4T hauls a rake mainly comprising SECR close-coupled suburban stock into the station. The stationmaster's house still looks new which suggests the photograph was taken shortly after 1906: the locality was still quite rural at that time. The main station building was rebuilt in the 1930s, like several others on the line, to cope with increased traffic as the area became built up. *Bexley Libraries & Museums Department*

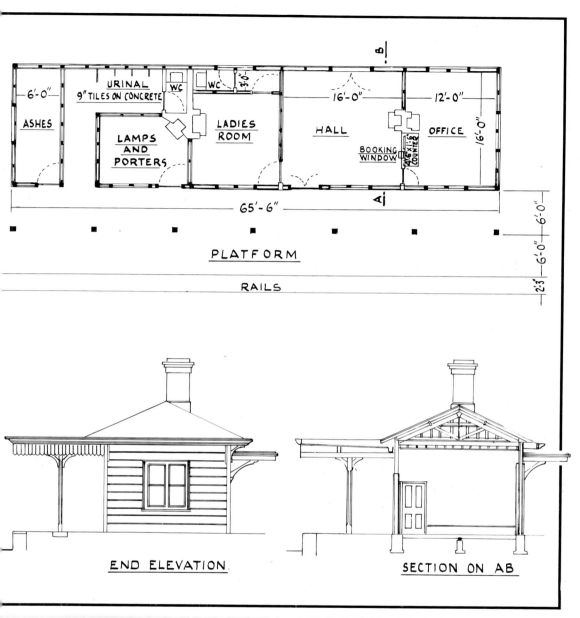

ASHES

6'-0"

URINAL
9" TILES ON CONCRETE

WC

WC

3'-0"

16'-0"

12'-0"

LAMPS
AND
PORTERS

LADIES
ROOM

HALL

16'-0"

OFFICE

BOOKING
WINDOW

4'-6"×1'-6"
COUNTER

B

A

65'-6"

6'-0"

6'-0"

2'-3"

PLATFORM

RAILS

END ELEVATION.

SECTION ON AB

2 Early Tudor and Vernacular Designs

In complete contrast to the undistinguished timber erections that formed the most numerous type of rural station on the SER were the various Tudor and Gothic designs particularly associated with the Strood–Paddock Wood line, the Tunbridge Wells–Hastings line and the Redhill and Reading line, all of which were built between 1844 and 1856.

Precursors of the Tudor style were the three stations built at Wye, Chartham and Grove Ferry in 1846. Wye had tee-shaped buildings with a two storey station-master's house at right angles to the railway and a single storey waiting room with attic above. Its outline was most picturesque with steeply pitched roofs, broken by gables and tall chimneys. Built of red brick, its appearance was further enhanced by stone quoins and capping. Grove Ferry bore a family resemblance but both portions were two storeyed and slightly less elaborate in their design. Chartham was smaller still, a rather nondescript single storey structure.

The stations on the Redhill–Reading line opened in 1849 were far more spectacular, and they included Reigate, Betchworth, Dorking Town, Chilworth, Shalford, Wokingham, Blackwater and Ash. The most attractive were the tiled and half-timbered stations between Redhill and Guildford. Betchworth, Chilworth and Shalford were each different in shape and layout but maintained a common picturesque outline and made effective use of vernacular materials – a warm red brick and weather tiles on the walls. The Tudor theme was evident in the jettied upper storeys, massive chimney stacks and large gables, very much a reflection of the prevailing style for country house lodges in South East England. Later alterations to the buildings were made sympathetically and did not detract from their appearance. In contrast to the asymmetrical designs favoured for the smaller stations, Reigate and Dorking Town had symmetrical twin gabled buildings of generally similar design. Both had delicate fretwork bargeboards under the gable eaves while Dorking had decorative half timbering applied.

Gomshall & Shere, unlike the other stations on this stretch of line, had a classical building, as did Ash, while Wokingham and Blackwater reverted to a picturesque Tudor outline, though quite different in style to the tile hung variety. The walls were enlivened by the use of diapered brickwork in the Tudor manner on the gable ends. Crowthorne, opened as Wellington College, acquired a station much later in 1859, but the Tudor Gothic style was utilised again with most impressive first floor windows with Gothic pointed tops to them and elaborate barge boarding.

Below left:
The picturesque station at Wye in the 1950s. The window set in the chimney stack is something that by all conventional building rules ought not to happen.
Lens of Sutton

Right:
A very Kentish scene. Surrounded by oasthouses and with fruit trees growing behind the down platform, Chartham station awaits the approaching train c1903. A smaller contemporary of Wye, Chartham later acquired standard SER shelters. The oil lamps are mounted at a low height on short wooden posts. *Lens of Sutton*

Below right:
The same station in the 1960s looking towards Canterbury, giving a better view of the station buildings and signalbox. The gabled crossing keeper's cottage is of a pattern found along this stretch of line. The walls of the cottages were usually painted black with quoins, window surrounds and bargeboards picked out in white or cream, a pleasing effect. A pre-cast concrete footbridge of the usual SR type has recently been added.
J. L. Smith

Below:
Grove Ferry, another delightful station in a superb rural setting; immediately behind the station is the ferry over the River Stour from which it derived its name. A crossing keeper's cottage similar to that at Chartham is at the Canterbury end of the station, together with one of the early signal huts now used for controlling the level crossing. A horsebox sits in a road reached by a wagon turntable. *Lens of Sutton*

Below:
Another view of Grove Ferry, looking in the opposite direction, with the staggered platforms evident. An SER round ended open is in the down siding, and the station staff pose with milk cans as props while the two small boys look on. Iron railings of the type seen here are more typical of the LCDR, the SER favouring wooden fencing.
G. L. Gundry Collection

Right:
Betchworth was one of the charming small stations on the Redhill–Guildford line built in the Surrey vernacular style in 1849. Tile hung with large gables and massive chimney stacks, it resembles an estate cottage and survives largely intact, this photograph being taken in 1980.

Bottom:
As befitted an important market town, Dorking received a much larger station building, twin gabled with half timbering in place of the tile hanging. The canopy is a much later addition, as is the subway which with its rounded corrugated iron roof is another typical SER feature. Everything in this c1960 photograph, save for the subway, has now gone. *J. L. Smith*

Above:
Chilworth, seen here in 1936 looking towards Guildford, was generally similar to Betchworth and was extended sympathetically in 1893. A small Railway Signal Co box lies beyond the waiting shelter. While the SER bracket signal remained, the Southern Railway's influences may be seen in the raising of the platforms with pre-cast concrete components. *H. A. Vallance*

Below:
Perhaps the most attractive of all the neo-Tudor stations was Shalford, and this fine postcard view of c1910 looking towards Dorking reveals a mass of detail. The loggia under the front gable was both unusual and charming. The cattle dock was located right by a point – if a railway modeller did this he would be told immediately that it was not prototypical! Neither, for that matter, was the absence of a buffer stop to the siding. Goods facilities are quite lavish in the shape of a 'roader' shed and a large warehouse. *Lens of Sutton*

Above:
Wellington College (Crowthorne from 1928), a much later building dating from 1859 but still maintaining a family resemblance to the earlier tile hung stations through the delicate bargeboarding. The row of dormers with appropriately pointed windows are particularly impressive. *Lens of Sutton*

Below:
The Italianate station at Gomshall & Shere was in complete contrast to its neighbours and was in effect a twin gabled version of Winchelsea or Ham Street. In this photograph of c1873 the resemblance is clear, but the fitting of a canopy extending the length of the building, the replacement of the small windows on the first floor with conventional sashes and the painting of the brickwork in later years tended to disguise it. *Lens of Sutton*

3 The Tunbridge Wells–Hastings–Ashford Line Stations

Another superb series of stations were those on the Hastings line and beyond to Ashford opened in 1851. The architect for some of these was William Tress of Wilson Street, Fitzroy Square, London whose name appears on a number of original drawings for the stations. Frant, Etchingham and Battle were Gothic; Wadhurst, Ticehurst Road (later Stonegate) and Robertsbridge were Italianate. The Italianate style continued on the Ashford line with the stations at Winchelsea, Rye, Ham Street and Appledore.

As a whole, this group of stations was perhaps the finest of the period in Southern England. All still exist and have not suffered undue mutilation in recent years. They form a remarkable contrast to the timber erections put up both before and after 1851, often serving much more important places, for example Bromley North and Sevenoaks.

Taking the stations in line order, Frant was a charming asymmetrical structure of stone with a highly decorative tiled roof. Originally the smaller gable had a bay window on the platform side, lighting the booking office, but this was removed when the building was extended in length and fitted with an awning in 1905. The alterations were carried out very sympathetically, great care being taken to match materials and proportions – a characteristic feature of the SER which usually specified that the contractor was to make every effort to blend new work in with the old.

Wadhurst in complete contrast was a pure Italianate station, beautifully proportioned in warm red brick, the effect set off by stone mouldings around the windows and a dentilled cornice. Cream brick quoins and a small pediment also contributed to the illusion of a small country house. The symmetry was spoilt by a later first floor addition containing an extra bedroom.

Ticehurst Road was another excursion in Italianate but completely different to Wadhurst. It was a little fussy in its detail, perhaps more typically Victorian than Wadhurst which maintained a Georgian delicacy in its proportions. However, it was no less attractive for that. For many years the brickwork was painted a dark colour to contrast with the light coloured quoins and mouldings. The present practice of painting all the building white does little for the station's appearance.

Etchingham was built in similar Tudor Gothic style to Frant but was considerably extended in 1864 and the platform elevation was transformed by an unusually deep canopy in 1914.

Robertsbridge had a most distinctive Italianate station. Asymmetrical in design, it had a two storey stationmaster's residence flanked on either side by single storey additions forming the booking office and staff accommodation Entry to the building from the forecourt was through an elegant loggia of three arches which were reflected in the rounded tops to

Below:
Often described as the finest small Gothic station in the country, Battle was a remarkably successful attempt to build in harmony with the nearby Abbey. The station is seen here in 1872 before the addition of a canopy spoilt the platform elevation. Early English arches provide protection from the weather outside the booking office, while the ecclesiastical theme is carried through to the extent of having a belfry. The station layout is the usual arrangement of staggered platforms and signal hut.
Lens of Sutton

many of the windows. The roof of the booking office was extended to shelter passengers on the platform. Corners and string courses were laid with white bricks to give a polychrome effect.

The pièce de résistance of the line was Battle, architecturally one of the most important country stations to be built. Designed by Tress to harmonise with its historic setting, it was constructed of coursed rubble in a very pure Gothic style. The tracery of the booking office windows conformed to the Decorated style, the house windows were Early English lancets and the timber roof of the booking office was more akin to that of a church. The ecclesiastical associations were heightened by the inclusion of two Gothic arches on the platform side, unfortunately obscured by the building of an awning in the latter part of the 19th century. The smaller gable on the platform side had a cross, while abutting the gable was a small belfry. An adjoining bay window was subsequently removed although most of the material was reused. The attractive stone walls were complemented by

roofs tiled in alternate bands of plain and fishscale tiles surmounted by decorative ridging.

Winchelsea and Ham Street were built to similar design, a simple Italianate with low pitched roofs and broad eaves. An attractive feature was a canopy extending around three sides of the building, roofed in slate to match the main roof, a rare instance of a canopy looking as though it was part of the initial design rather than an afterthought. The small Brunel stations on the Great Western Railway were some of the relatively few examples of successfully integrated canopies that spring to mind.

Rye had an imposing station as befits its status. A symmetrical arrangement of a recessed centre flanked by two wings with a loggia under three arches on the forecourt side gave it a dignified appearance. The central recessed portion on the platform side was higher than the wings. Rusticated quoins contributed to the imposing effect, as did the corbelling on the first floor cornice. Stone string courses enlivened the cheerful red brick of the facade.

Above:
Robertsbridge looking south on 26 July 1888. Better known in later years as the junction for the Kent & East Sussex Railway, the station is of considerable interest in its own right. A goodly supply of SER detail is visible: the boarded fence, the roader shed and the early signalbox. The handsome Italianate station building is complemented by a matching crossing keeper's house, while trailing ivy adds an additional note of domesticity to the main building. In the yard at the rear is the goods warehouse which, dating from 1851 (the same year as the station), is of the pattern used all along the line.
Lens of Sutton

Right:
The road frontage at Battle is equally picturesque. The large windows in the Decorated style contrast with the Early English lancets. The building, here photographed on 15 April 1984, has suffered few changes over the years on the road side, the simplification of the chimneys being the most notable. The decorative ironwork along the capping and the tiles themselves are original. A highly commendable point is that the exterior has not been disfigured by posters or even a British Rail sign.

Top:
A group of jolly young men stroll up Station Road, Robertsbridge. The Ostrich Hotel (proprietor, E. J. Waghorn), which was the station hotel, still survives but the gate keeper's cottage on the left has gone. The cottage has had its brickwork covered by slate tiles to keep the rain out. *G. L. Gundry Collection*

Above:
This photograph of 15 April 1984 of the road side elevation reveals the considerable size of Robertsbridge station, considering the community it served. The loggia by the entrance is an attractive and unusual detail. Note the variety in window forms.

Right:
At Etchingham a reversion was made to stone construction, this time in the Tudor style as opposed to the very plausible attempt at Gothic at Battle. This is basically the original structure but much extended on the left in 1864 and fitted with the present canopy in 1914, the excessively deep valancing of which blends unhappily with the rest of the building. Photographed 15 April 1984.

Top:
Ticehurst Road, later known as Stonegate, looking towards Tunbridge Wells in the 1880s. The dog joins the station staff in posing for the photographer. Continuing in the Italianate vein of Robertsbridge, the building is largely as built although an extra bedroom has been provided on the first floor. The job of matching the new work with the old has been so skilfully done, the change is not immediately apparent. As in so many of these stations, a roader shed has been provided.
Lens of Sutton

Above:
A rear view displays the combination of the symmetry of Wadhurst's facade and the variety of window forms as employed at Robertsbridge to good effect. The brickwork has been painted white which has meant that much of the contrast between the rich natural shades of the brick and the quoins, pediment and other decorative features is lost. Photographed 15 April 1984.

Left:
Wadhurst is, in my opinion, the most attractive of the Italianate stations. It is shown here in the 1870s looking towards Tunbridge Wells. All the familiar elements in the SER scene are present.   *Lens of Sutton*

Top:
Wadhurst on 6 September 1969. The previously symmetrical station building has had a bedroom added in a matching style, a first floor window has been enlarged and the fine pediment simplified. A Dutton signalbox replaced the earlier structure in 1893. A standard SECR footbridge stands in place of the simple foot crossing. *J. Scrace*

Above:
The road side of Wadhurst was equally attractive. It is seen in this view of c1910 which shows the unusual yard layout with a siding running across the station approach road into a separate coal depot belonging to Cheesman & Newington, Coal, Coke & Manure Merchants. The goods warehouse, visible in the background, is of the usual pattern for the line.
Lens of Sutton

Left:
Wadhurst goods yard with an '01' engaged in shunting a line of the characteristic round ended opens headed by a pair of SER brake vans. *Lens of Sutton*

S. E. R.

TONBRIDGE WELLS & HASTINGS.

WADHURST STATION.

Wadhurst station building prior to the addition of an extra bedroom on the first floor at the south end of the building. *Drawing by W. E. Rowley*

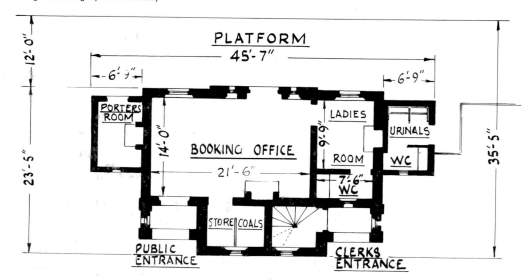

PLATFORM
45'-7"

PORTERS ROOM

BOOKING OFFICE
21'-6"

LADIES ROOM

URINALS

WC

7'-6" WC

STORE | COALS

PUBLIC ENTRANCE

CLERKS ENTRANCE

12'-0"

23'-5"

14'-0"

6'-7"

6'-9"

9'-9"

35'-5"

GROUND PLAN

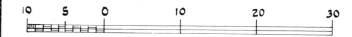

10   5   0   10   20   30

Right:
A superb general view of the station, looking very trim c1910. Note how the early signalbox has survived side by side with its replacement. Posters for Dover and, more romantically, Monte Carlo adorn the box.
Lens of Sutton

Far right:
Frant was a pretty, small building that was extensively altered and enlarged over the years. The first additions were made in 1859 and a bedroom was added in 1884, forming the third gable from the left in the photograph. The near end of the building was altered, the wall on the platform side heightened and the canopy fitted in 1905. This picture taken in August 1936, shows the 1893 Saxby & Farmer signalbox after the Southern Railway had reduced the depth of the locking room storey.
H. A. Vallance

30

PLATFORM ELEVATION

LEVEL OF RAILS

FRONT ELEVATION

LEVEL OF PLATFORM

LEVEL OF GROUND

Above:
A recent view of Frant, in April 1984. The fabric of the building has changed little and is still in good condition.

Below:
Rye was the grandest of the Italianate stations and complemented well the architectural beauty of the town it served. Designed by William Tress and built in 1851, it is seen here in 1947 with the columns of its elegant loggia still disfigured by the zebra stripes used in World War 2. The parcels office is a sympathetic addition by the Southern Railway. *LGRP, courtesy David & Charles*

Right:
Another variation on the South Eastern's Italianate theme, Ham Street, from a postcard c1905. The staff have put great efforts into their gardening; the entire length of the station as far as the boarded fence extends is lined with bushes and potted plants. Every window sill has a window box or pots while trailing plants grow up the walls. There are hints of even greater arboreal glories in the station master's garden beyond the fence. A good close up of one of the early signal cabins on the left and of the oil lamps that still remained (albeit non-operative) when I visited the station in 1974 are other points of interest. *Lens of Sutton*

4 Tudor Stations of 1856

Three more stations to the same high standard as the Tress designs on the Hastings line were those at Cuxton, Aylesford and Wateringbury. Cuxton and Aylesford were opened with the Strood–Maidstone line in 1856, and Wateringbury is believed to have been rebuilt the same year.

Cuxton was the smallest of the three, mainly single storey with a two storey residence at the rear. Constructed of brick it had decorative tiling, fine chimneys of a great height and stone mullions around the windows, which had charming frames of latticed ironwork, a feature unique to this line. The overall effect was that of a lodge by the gates of a great country house.

Aylesford was, if anything, even more spectacular. Rather larger, being of two storeys throughout, its booking office was lit by three tall windows on the platform side. What made it stand out from other stations in the area was the use of local ragstone for the walls, a material that gave it a wonderful silvery appearance in sunlight. The same style was used on neighbouring crossing keepers' cottages to good effect.

Wateringbury was originally almost identical to Aylesford, save for it being constructed of red brick instead of ragstone, with stonework extensively used for quoins and lintels. The house was skilfully enlarged in 1899 to provide an extra bedroom.

All three stations still exist. Wateringbury is especially worth a visit, with an idyllic location beside the River Medway. It is still an intact rural station complete with waiting shed, goods shed, signalbox and a separate stationmaster's house. The illusion is only spoilt by the way in which a substantial portion of the south end of the station building was removed circa 1970.

Below:
The charming Tudor station at Aylesford looking towards Maidstone c1910. Again, the skill with which additions were blended in with the existing building is apparent as the first floor as far as the second drainpipe had only been built a few years previously in 1901. The crossing keeper's cottage was, like the station, put up in 1856 and was in a matching style, as was a similar structure at nearby Mill Hill Crossing. All three buildings still exist today. The tall SER signal has Coligny Welch indicators on the distant arms and also has repeater arms due to the footbridge obscuring the view ahead. *Lens of Sutton*

Above:
Aylesford in the 1950s, showing the great height of the elaborate lattice window frames. It is a pity that the SECR did not try to match these when adding the bedroom to the left of the picture. *Lens of Sutton*

Above right:
The down platform at Wateringbury in the 1930s. The shelter has gained some valancing in late SECR days but otherwise the scene remains unchanged from what it was 30 years earlier. The Saxby & Farmer signalbox of 1894 and the goods warehouse still exist.
Lens of Sutton

Below:
Wateringbury was built to a similar design to Aylesford but in brick rather than stone. Two varieties of SER platform seat of spindly appearance and a wall mounted oil lamp are prominent in this c1910 view.
Lens of Sutton

Right:
Wateringbury always appeared a more impressive structure than Aylesford, due to its having been extended on several occasions to form a long range of buildings. The earliest part, dating from 1856, is to the left, a bedroom was added on the first floor c1886 and a third addition, that furthest from the camera, was added in 1899. *Lens of Sutton*

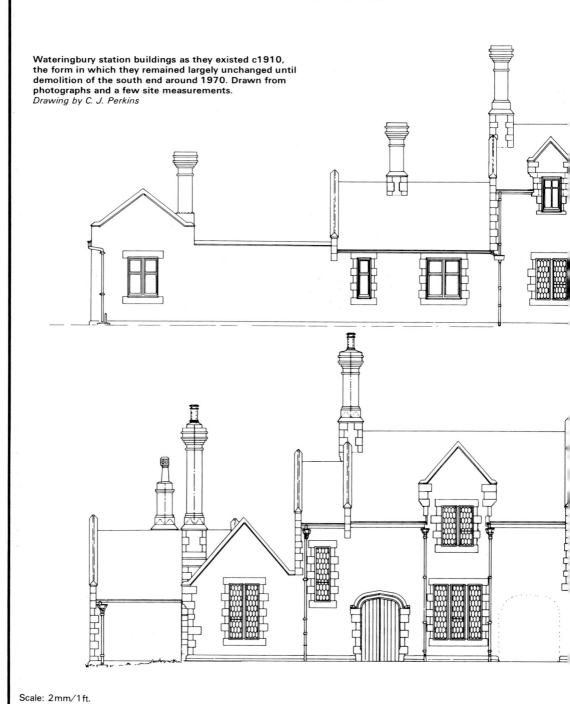

Wateringbury station buildings as they existed c1910, the form in which they remained largely unchanged until demolition of the south end around 1970. Drawn from photographs and a few site measurements.
Drawing by C. J. Perkins

Scale: 2mm/1ft.

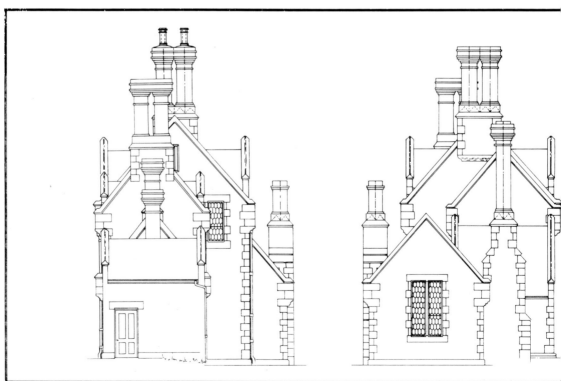

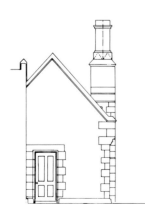

Above left:
The elevations of Wateringbury are equally attractive from the approach road. The furthermost building is the station cottage which completed the row. Photographed 19 April 1981.

Above:
Cuxton, the third station in the Tudor style on the Strood–Paddock Wood line, was less spectacular but still well supplied with the fine detailing that characterised its neighbours. Seen here in Edwardian days, the bracketed down starter frames the view northwards.
Lens of Sutton

Below:
The modern lighting and the ugly wire fence succeed in detracting a little from the charm of Cuxton station today but it retains its picturesque outline. Photographed 23 April 1984.

5 Individual Designs

There were quite a number of one-off buildings, some to a high architectural standard, others decidedly not. The reasons for these individual designs being used are by no means clear in the majority of cases.

Sturry was one such undistinguished building, a very small hipped roofed brick box with a centre portion flanked by two smaller wings. In other respects the station was a normal wayside depot with staggered platforms. A level crossing between the two platforms effectively dividing the station into two halves was an unusual feature, however.

Another station serving a very small community, Smeeth, had a rather more impressive structure. Although totally unlike any other building on the SER, it was of a type found in other parts of the country. It was composed of three single storey gabled portions linked together. Part of these were rendered, part left in their natural brick. As if this accommodation was not more than adequate, a timber waiting shed with most unusual windows, round topped within rectangular frames, was added.

The next station down the main line, Westenhanger, was equally odd in its way. A sizeable and imposing, if not especially attractive, house set at right angles to the track with a large porch on the road side (although the word drive would seem more appropriate), it was the very epitome of a mid-Victorian gentleman's detached villa. There is no question of the railway having converted an existing dwelling as the house clearly post-dates the opening of the line. A platform wall in matching yellow brick gave the station a unified appearance.

A very fine classical station was erected at Snodland in 1856. It was quite unlike any other station in the vicinity, the remaining stations on the line being Tudor. Constructed of red brick with perfectly symmetrical elevations, its detailing was particularly careful. White brick quoins on the corners and around door openings provided variety in surface texture. Why such an imposing building was erected at a small town remains a mystery. The station remains largely intact, the only major alteration being the partial replacement of the original simple canopy and the fitting of valancing.

The joint line between Deal and Dover, opened in 1881, produced two substantial single storey brick buildings at Walmer and Martin Mill. Although the line was joint, the stations were pure South Eastern. Walmer was the larger of the two and considerably more elaborate than its neighbour, the principal distinguishing feature being prominent corbels. It was very similar in style to Folkestone West, also opened in 1881. Awnings were of the usual SER pattern with rounded tops, and both stations were provided with the characteristic subways favoured by the company in its later years.

North Camp near Aldershot acquired a new station in 1863, which had a decidedly suburban look to it. A large single storey structure with a central portion flanked by two wings, it was in the cruder Italianate much favoured by the nearby LSWR at this period in such stations as Norbiton, Gunnersbury and, indeed, Aldershot itself. The substantial accommodation was increased by the addition of a refreshment room, very much in the manner of Kew Gardens, probably run by the Railway Hotel which stood in close proximity and was similar in style. This quite extensive provision of facilities was most likely occasioned by the military traffic passing through the station. The general style of North Camp was to be followed by others, including the stations at Hither Green and Chislehurst, rebuilt as late as 1901 in a style which was by then some 40 years out of date.

What amounted to brick versions of the standard wooden station were put up at Halling (1890), Yalding (1894), Farnborough North (1889) and Coulsdon South (1889). All had the usual half round roofs on the canopies which were mounted on iron posts at Farnborough and Yalding and wood at the other two stations. Higham acquired a similar building, but which was fitted with only a very small canopy. Lacking the naturally attractive finish that timber cladding provides, these brick stations looked very drab. Farnborough North, in common with many other stations on the Reading line, has had its buildings replaced by bus shelters.

Other brick buildings of little distinction compared to the architectural glories of earlier years were provided at Brooklands Halt and Lydd Town in 1881 and New Romney in 1884. All three were built to different designs. Brooklands had large accommodation for its isolated location with two platforms and a fair sized station building complete with quoins and bargeboards. It was part rendered and presented a piebald appearance. The original terminus of the branch had what can only be described as a timber shack with only the lighthouse and its keepers' cottages for company. The platform was faced with timber in the best light railway tradition although the branch was not in fact one.

Two stations built to the same design in 1883 and 1888 respectively were those at Nutfield and Sandling. These were unquestionably two of the finest stations the SER produced and, indeed, rank among the best examples of the English domestic revival as applied to railway stations, along with the T.H. Myres stations on the LBSCR and numerous examples built on the GER up to the turn of the century. Why the SER built just these two examples only at a time when much of its building was in the pleasant but unremarkable timber style is not known, but it is a great shame that it was not perpetuated.

The design was impressive in its simplicity. Brick walls were divided by half timbering applied to produce simple rectangles, while windows were fitted neatly into some of the rectangles so produced. The roofs were laid with tiles, steeply pitched and half hipped at the ends. Over the booking hall entrance on the road side was a gabled porch, perfectly proportioned in relation to the rest of the building so that it provided the finishing touch rather than, as so often happened, looking like an unfortunate afterthought.

Gone was the usual valance, leaving the main supporting beam and brackets exposed to view, rather in the manner of some early stations on other railways of the 1840s. The overall impression was of a clean, unfussy design. The main building at Sandling was by the Sandgate branch platforms. It has now been demolished but the slightly smaller building constructed in a matching style on the up main line platform still survives. At Nutfield, a matching signalbox was provided to complete the illusion of an architect designed station. Nutfield was sadly demolished in the 1970s 'purge' on the Reading line.

Although a major railway junction in the Weald, Paddock Wood was little more than a village when the railway was opened and indeed the station was originally called Maidstone Road.

Above:
The first view, taken in 1872, shows the station very much as it must have appeared when first constructed. The SER planned its early stations on a generous scale with through roads. The handsome Italianate building on the down side is the original of 1842, as yet unsullied by awnings. The footbridge has on the down side an impressive clock tower, rather in the manner of Tunbridge Wells.   *Lens of Sutton*

Above right:
The same scene c1912. The two views give a good idea of typical changes that occurred in a station over 40 years. Platforms have been lengthened, awnings (or 'covered ways' as the SER referred to them) have been added and sheds have sprouted. The flimsy looking iron footbridge has been replaced by something conforming to similar lines but rather more substantial.
Lens of Sutton

Right:
A general view of Paddock Wood looking in the opposite direction showing the up side which was rebuilt in 1893. A large signal gantry stands over the down slow road. In a siding at the rear of the station are a line of what were known as Vacuum Thirds. These were early examples of something the Southern became very adept at producing: old bodies on new underframes. In this case, two old four wheel bodies built mainly between 1860 and 1863 were fitted on to new six wheel chassis between 1893 and 1895.   *Lens of Sutton*

Top:
A dignified rural station: Westenhanger in 1879. The original signalbox stands opposite its hipped roof replacement while the goods shed is in an unusual position (for the SER), opposite the main station building. Three single bolsters are in the process of having some tree trunks roped to them. *Lens of Sutton*

Above:
A much later photograph of Westenhanger (c1910) shows the considerable number of staff to be found at a small station. A third signalbox to Evans O'Donnell design has been built and an ancient carriage grounded on the right; otherwise the scene is little changed. *Lens of Sutton*

Right:
Westenhanger today is boarded up and has a 'To Let' sign outside. This was the entrance to the booking office and the position of the imposing porch is clearly to be seen in the brickwork. Photographed 3 June 1984.

Top:
The restrained classical station at Snodland. The valancing added to the canopies was the only significant alteration to have occurred since construction in this c1910 view. *Lens of Sutton*

Above:
A 1950s view of the road side of Snodland. *J. L. Smith*

Left:
The platform side of Snodland today, photographed 23 April 1984.

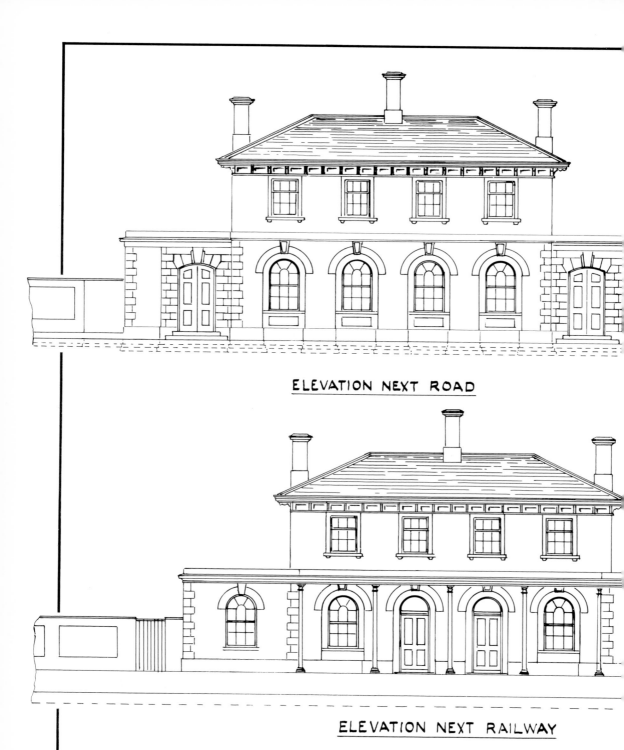

ELEVATION NEXT ROAD

ELEVATION NEXT RAILWAY

Snodland station buildings as built. The only major
change has been the reconstruction of the canopy.
Drawing by W. E. Rowley

Scale: 2mm/1ft.

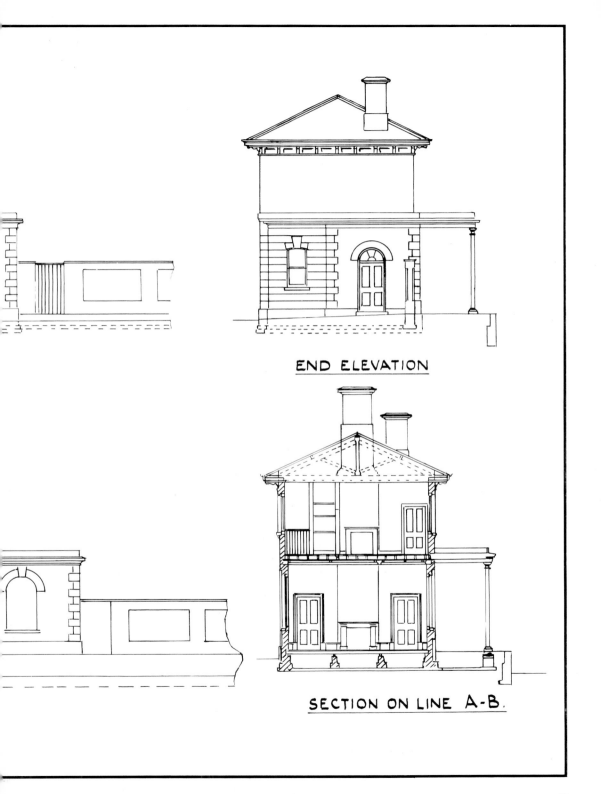

END ELEVATION

SECTION ON LINE A-B.

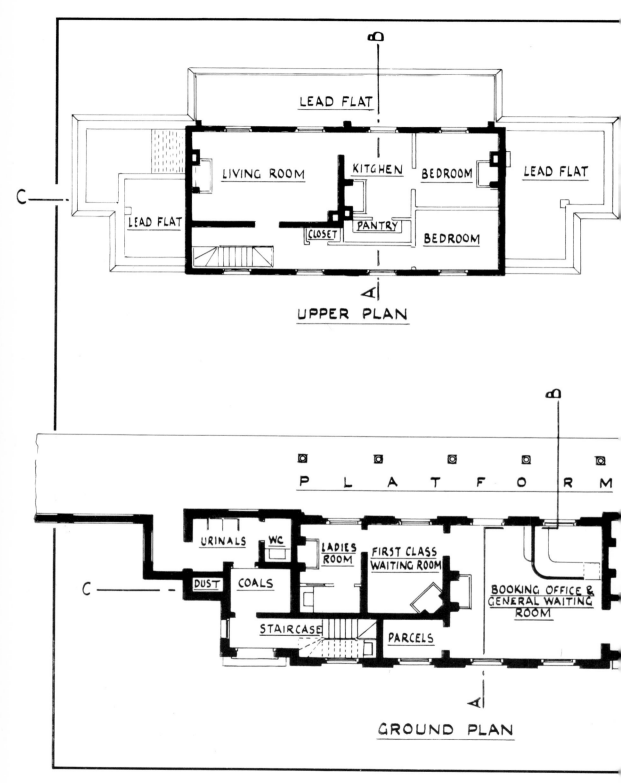

LEAD FLAT

LIVING ROOM

KITCHEN

BEDROOM

LEAD FLAT

LEAD FLAT

CLOSET

PANTRY

BEDROOM

C

UPPER PLAN

PLATFORM

URINALS

WC

LADIES ROOM

FIRST CLASS WAITING ROOM

BOOKING OFFICE & GENERAL WAITING ROOM

DUST

COALS

C

STAIRCASE

PARCELS

GROUND PLAN

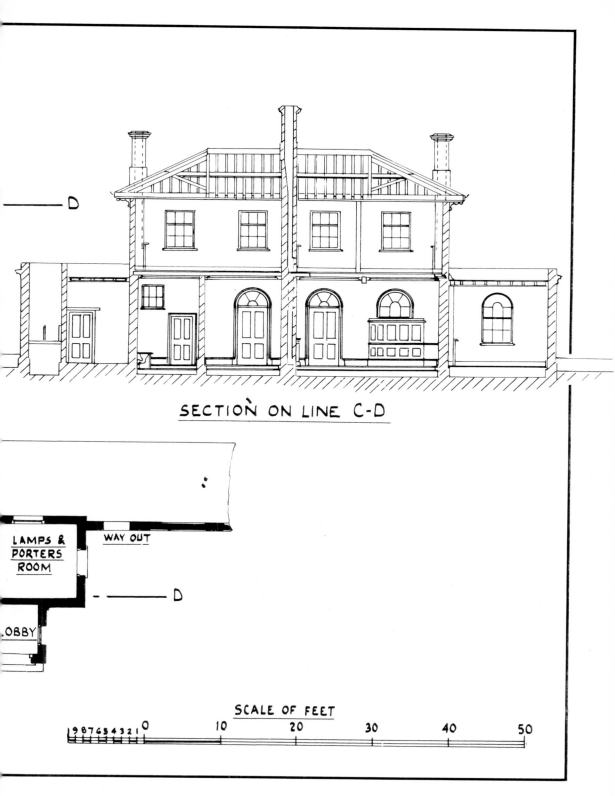

SECTION ON LINE C-D

LAMPS &
PORTERS
ROOM

WAY OUT

D

LOBBY

SCALE OF FEET

9 8 7 6 5 4 3 2 1 0   10   20   30   40   50

Above:
Aldershot North Camp was a wayside station with a considerable military traffic and the buildings were rebuilt in the 1860s to deal more effectively with it. This view of the station building c1960 shows the vivid polychromatic effect obtained by the use of red brick panels and arches on a yellow stock brick background. *J. L. Smith*

Below:
Another view of North Camp depicting the platform elevations and Saxby & Farmer signalbox (since demolished). *J L Smith*

Above right:
A roadside view of Halling in the 1950s. *J. L. Smith*

Right:
Higham, looking towards Gravesend, a particularly plain example of the relatively few small brick wayside stations. The canopy does not extend the full length of the building but only over the entrance. The overbridge in the background is a reminder that this stretch of railway was built on the course of the Thames & Medway Canal. *Lens of Sutton*

Below right:
The remaining examples of the type were slightly more generous in their protection for the passenger. Halling c1905 has the standard SER shelter on the down side and a flat roofed roader shed as opposed to the usual gabled design. *Lens of Sutton*

Above left:
Yalding had an identical building to Halling. It is seen here c1908 with the Saxby & Farmer style signalbox erected 1894, the same year as the station was rebuilt. The name plate of the box – Yalding Station Signals – shows up well in contrast to the LCDR's use of the word 'Box'. The lamp mounted on the signal post is worthy of note, as are the vertical palings of the level crossing gate. *Lens of Sutton*

Left:
The scene at Yalding is little changed today as this picture taken on 19 April 1981 shows.

Above:
Farnborough North in 1949, another example of the type, replaced c1970 with a bus stop shelter. The signalbox is of Railway Signal Co design.
LGRP, courtesy David & Charles

Below:
Coulsdon South differed from the other stations of this type by having a waiting shelter matching the canopy on the station building. 'Gladstone' No 195 hauls a down train. *Lens of Sutton*

Above:

Smeeth, looking towards Ashford, c1904. Situated some way from any centres of population, quite extensive accommodation was nonetheless provided.
Lens of Sutton

Below:

Another view of Smeeth, taken on a wet day shortly before closure in 1954, shows the unusual gabled buildings. The third gable was a later addition, probably in the late 1860s. One of the SER's highly individualistic home grown signalboxes is adjacent. This one has windows positioned almost at random with no regard for aesthetics whatsoever. *J. L. Smith*

Right:

An up express hauled by 'D' class No 747 pulls out of Sandling Junction c1910. The Sandgate branch train is standing by the down branch platform, and is composed of ex-LCDR six wheeled stock with an ex-SER brake van. To the right is the principal station building.
Lens of Sutton

Below right:

The superb station at Nutfield in the 1950s. Note how the signalbox reflects the neo-vernacular charm of the station buildings. It is a pity that a matching waiting shed, instead of the standard structure, was not provided. *J. L. Smith*

6 Corrugated Iron Stations – Hawkhurst Branch and Elham Valley Lines

These two branches are treated together as their stations have much in common. The engineer of the Cranbrook & Paddock Wood Railway built a line that would not have been out of place in Umbria, climbing as it did along the steep sides of a narrow valley, verdant with hops and fruit trees, until reaching a terminus in the middle of nowhere one mile north of Hawkhurst.

The stations were very similar to those employed by Colonel Stephens on his light railways some years later. They were small corrugated iron affairs whose pitched roofs extended to form a canopy on the platform side where they rested on simple wooden posts. Horsmonden and Hawkhurst were of this most basic type; at Cranbrook and Goudhurst the design was refined to include a three storey brick house attached to the end of the iron buildings. These houses were tall and thin, the height being accentuated by dormers and small windows. The combination of these oddly proportioned houses and the shed-like booking offices cannot be said to be a happy one.

Cranbrook had a particularly fine position; located on a gentle curve, it was set in the hills in such a way that it was almost framed by them: it would make a beautiful model. It survives today as a private residence, complete with goods shed and signalbox. The lever frame was, I believe, removed in the 1960s and deposited outside the box as a piece of abstract sculpture! Horsmonden too still remains recognisable,

in use with a local garage. Goudhurst has vanished completely, while at Hawkhurst the signalbox and engine shed are in good condition but the station itself has gone.

The Elham Valley line was one of the most obscure railways in Southern England. Photographs of it are rare and until recently it had completely escaped the attentions of the railway press. The stations at Canterbury South, Bishopsbourne and Bridge all had identical buildings, very similar to those on the Hawkhurst branch except that they were slightly shorter – four supports to the canopy instead of five. The remaining two stations, Lyminge and Elham, were of the usual timber style and have been mentioned in Chapter 1.

Above:
Goudhurst c1960 showing the brick stationmaster's house attached to the corrugated iron building. The house too is no architectural masterpiece. *J. L Smith*

Below:
The utilitarian style employed on the Hawkhurst branch: Horsmonden was the smallest example of this unlovely design. A boy waits with his dog while the portly gentleman to his left appears to be sitting on his four legged friend. The construction of the station is well displayed; it could scarcely be simpler. The location of Horsmonden was delightful, being situated on the edge of the village, surrounded by oast houses and a mill.
Lens of Sutton

The London Chatham & Dover Railway

The station erected at Shepherds Well in 1861 was in general not unlike the first EKR batch. In this c1903 view it has acquired the slightly ramshackle air that seems to have befallen some of the LCDR stations: the company's practice of siting enamelled advertisements wherever there was a vacant piece of wall available may have contributed. The station's name is given on a small sign above that for Ashes Ales and Stouts; the steps down from the platform to the crossing are unusual. The seat on the up platform with its shapely cast legs is of a type frequently used on the LCDR, while the waiting shed beyond is of the early type similar to that at Teynham. *Lens of Sutton*

7 Stations

London Chatham & Dover Railway stations were far more uniform in appearance than those on the South Eastern Railway, which is perhaps not surprising in that we are discussing designs over a 40-year period rather than the 60 years during which the SER built most of its stations. The company had the great misfortune to come into being at a time when architectural standards for small stations were generally in decline and also to remain chronically poor throughout its existence. Most of the stations are generally unadorned to the point of being plain, although the company always had a liking for polychromy, strongly evidenced in the stations on the Maidstone–Ashford line.

To the company's credit, the vast majority of stations were built of brick rather than wood, generally in variations on the theme of a two storey stationmaster's house linked to a single storey booking office. All had awnings to shelter waiting passengers, regarded as essential by the 1860s.

East Kent Railway Designs

The wayside stations at Gillingham, Rainham and Teynham on the fledgling East Kent Railway, opened in 1858, were built to an identical design. They comprised substantial two storeyed houses with single storey extensions at each end. Small canopies, each with valancing, were provided at the front and rear. A feature of many of the stations built by the LCDR in its early years was the provision of a storm porch on the roadside under the canopy to keep draughts out of the booking office. Some were in brick and some were in wood. Those of brick often had wooden extensions built onto them with the result that every station presented a different appearance. The stations were built of yellow stock brick but most elevations were painted – if not from the outset, certainly by the early years of the present century. Decoration was reduced to a minimum; plain bargeboards and simple windows combined to give the stations a mean appearance, in keeping with the impecunious state of the company's finances. Gillingham and Rainham both survived into the early 1970s, and Teynham still exists, albeit in multilated form.

Below:
The archetypal East Kent Railway station, Teynham, looking towards Faversham c1905. Points worthy of note include the use of iron railings, the goods shed situated alongside the platform – covered with enamelled advertisements and having lamps suspended on brackets from it – and the station building with its brickwork painted. *Lens of Sutton*

Above right:
Another picture of the same period showing the down platform; the waiting shed is not original. The LCDR favoured small box-like structures but always embellished them with a simple valance.
Lens of Sutton

Right:
A view from the access road of Rainham station shows how these EKR structures were identical. Both the station and the warehouse beyond are as built except for a small timber extension to the booking office. The forecourt is enclosed by substantial gates while the SECR poster on the left advertises the 1912 Oxford and Cambridge boat race. *Lens of Sutton*

Below right:
Gillingham is certainly no longer a rural station but it was when opened in 1858 as the western terminus of the EKR. The original building, photographed in 1971, survived until the early 1970s and was identical in all major respects to the other stations of the type.

8 Early Brick Designs

Gables were large and overstated to obtain a picturesque effect in direct contrast to the mean, no frills approach employed earlier. Sevenoaks was different again: while at Eynsford the builder relied on form and proportion to achieve his desired results, at Sevenoaks he used decoration. Pointed tops to the windows, corbels and a vivid polychromy were to be the hallmarks of the LCDR for the rest of its existence, and Sevenoaks set the standard for the company's future style.

With the advance towards London in 1860 another design of country station appeared, no less austere and plain than those of two years previously. Stations to this design were erected at St Mary Cray, Farningham Road and Sole Street. The principal difference between them and the earlier type was that instead of being two storeyed throughout they comprised a single storey booking office attached to a two storey residence which did not have a gable facing the track. The dour appearance was not noticeably improved by painting the brickwork. All survive with the exception of St Mary Cray which was rebuilt in the 1930s.

A reversion to the earlier style was made in 1861 with the next stretch of line to be opened, that from Canterbury to Dover. Bekesbourne, Shepherds Well and Kearsney all had gables facing the platform and most of the brickwork painted. Bekesbourne and Shepherds Well were very similar and Kearsney (added in 1862) had a stationmaster's house of greater size. Adisham, however, had a station of the Farningham Road type.

Generally similar in shape but quite different in appearance were the stations at Eynsford and Sevenoaks Bat & Ball, built by the nominally independent Sevenoaks, Maidstone & Tunbridge Railway Co in 1862. Eynsford was a homely station with rendered elevations; Gothic treatment of the windows gave the building a most distinctive appearance.

Below:
Raising the platforms at Farningham Road in 1922. Looking towards Swanley, a good view of the principal buildings is obtained. On the right is the water tower which doubled up as a waiting room. The footbridge still exists although it has lost its roof, but the goods warehouse, which is similar to those erected at all the early LCDR stations, has been demolished.
H. J. Patterson Rutherford

Above right:
The exterior of Farningham Road, which differs from other LCDR stations of the period in that it lacks a canopy or porch by the booking office. Photographed 23 April 1984.

Right:
The platform side at Sole Street as seen on 23 April 1984. Generally, the building is in much better condition than Farningham Road of which it is almost a mirror image.

Below right:
Sole Street displays detail differences to Farningham Road. The entrance to the booking office is enclosed by a brick storm porch with a canopy giving further protection, and less of the brickwork is painted than at Farningham Road. The passage of time has resulted in a few changes; the window in the gable end nearest the camera has been bricked up and a new window inserted in the end wall of the stationmaster's house.

ELEVATION NEXT RAILWAY

9'-0"

10'-0"

ELEVATION NEXT ROAD APPROACH

5   10   20   25   30   35   40

E.K.R.

Above:
Adisham station building as constructed. A modification in LCDR days was a timber extension to the porch on the road side. *Drawing by W. E. Rowley*

Left:
Adisham was geographically isolated from the other buildings of this pattern, all the other examples being on the main line west of Rochester. The early oil lamps are noteworthy. *Lens of Sutton*

Right:
Adisham today is in a sadly decrepit state, although parts of the station have recently received a fresh coat of paint. Few major changes have occurred to the structure of the building and it conforms to the original drawing except that, as frequently happened, a timber extension has been added to the porch on the forecourt side.

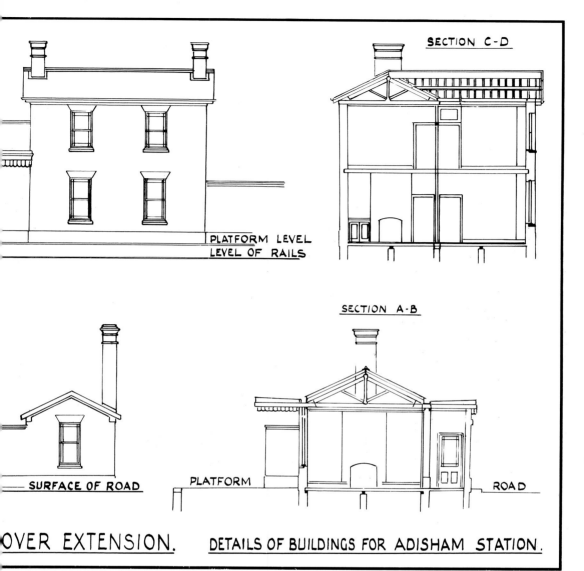

SECTION C-D

PLATFORM LEVEL
LEVEL OF RAILS

SECTION A-B

SURFACE OF ROAD

PLATFORM

ROAD

OVER EXTENSION.   DETAILS OF BUILDINGS FOR ADISHAM STATION.

PLAN ABOVE WINDOW CILLS

YARD — 20'-0" — 23'-6"

SCULLERY — 7'-0" — 11'-6"

PARLOUR — 13'-0"

KITCHEN — 11'-6" — 11'-6"

PAY OFFICE & GENERAL WAITING ROOM — 15'-0" — 18'-6" — 6'-4"

LADIES WAITING ROOM — 11'-6"

COVERERED WAY

Below:
A roadside view of Shepherds Well taken in 1933 which gives a good impression of the rather drab appearance of some of these early stations. Certainly the company's shareholders, whatever else they may have accused the Board of, could not complain of extravagence where stations were concerned. *LGRP, courtesy David & Charles*

Right:
Kearsney, looking towards Dover, in the late 1950s. A larger version of Shepherds Well, Kearsney was extended over the years. The gable nearest the camera housed an extra bedroom and was added in 1889 while the waiting shed on the down platform in front of the goods shed was built in 1882. *Lens of Sutton*

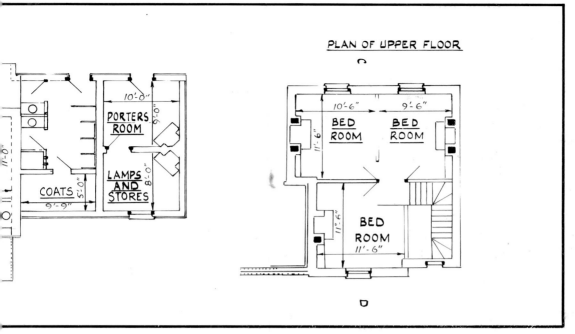

PLAN OF UPPER FLOOR

Above:
Eynsford gleams in the bright sunlight of a spring day in April 1984, resplendent in recently applied brown and cream paint. The highly ornamental treatment of the window sashes contrasts strongly with the plainness of the standard LCDR stations of the period.

Right:
Sevenoaks Bat & Ball in 1922 with the ridge of the North Downs in the background. The variety in the ownership of the open wagons on the left is notable; owners include LBSCR, SECR, GWR, GCR, CLC and L&Y. The track is still deeply ballasted at this comparatively late date. The signalbox is one of the LCDR's own design of the late 1870s while the timber structure in the foreground is the engine shed, reached via a turntable located adjacent to the station building.
H. J. Patterson Rutherford

Below:
The roadside elevation in August 1976. The exuberance of the polychromy is apparent while the extension of the roof in the centre to form a neat canopy is a feature rarely repeated.

9 Otford-Ashford Line Stations

A series of neat small stations was built on the Maidstone line at Kemsing, Wrotham & Borough Green, West Malling and Barming. These had a slightly recessed centre portion flanked by two gables and were constructed of a warm red brick replete with rusticated quoins. Usually they were not fitted with awnings. Barming is the only one still in original state as the remainder were rebuilt circa 1880.

On rebuilding at Wrotham & Borough Green and West Malling, one gable and the centre portion of the original building were retained and abutted the new station buildings. These were perhaps the most attractive built by the Chatham company. Constructed of a warm red brick enlivened by a restrained use of white brick on string courses and above window and door openings, the pointed windows gave them a Gothic flavour. Two storeyed throughout with a projecting gable at one end, the roof line was punctuated with four small gables on both road and platform sides, each with miniature bargeboards. The resultant accommodation for the stationmaster was spacious indeed. Canopies with unusually deep valancing were provided on the platform side and more conventional valancing on the roadside.

Both of these fine stations are still extant and West Malling benefits from a superb location some way out of the town it serves, and from which it is approached along a sweeping driveway through the fields.

The final set of rural stations built by the LCDR were those on the extension of the Maidstone line to a new terminus at Ashford in 1884. Buildings in the most vivid polychrome brick were erected at Bearsted and Thurnham, Hollingbourne, Harrietsham, Lenham, Charing and Hothfield.

The combination of white brickwork highlighted with bright red in horizontal bands and over openings and gables at Bearsted, Hollingbourne and Harrietsham is still as vivid as it must have been when new due to the clean country air. In contrast Lenham, Charing and Hothfield were built of red brick picked out in bands of darker red. All still exist today with the exception of Hothfield.

Below:
The extension from Otford Junction to Maidstone, opened in 1874, had neat brick twin gabled stations of which Barming is the only survivor in original form. Note the use of local ragstone for facing the platform. Photographed 22 May 1971. *J. Scrace*

Above left:
In this picture of Malling c1905 the single storey portion to the right is two-thirds of the 1874 station, and beyond is the large and decorative building of 1880.
Lens of Sutton

Left:
The road side elevation of Malling is equally impressive. The use of these gables is unique to this line. The iron railings favoured by the LCDR are much in evidence. Photographed 23 April 1984.

Above:
Wrotham & Borough Green, another example of the 1880 station rebuildings. The photo is taken looking towards London with the gable of the original building just visible beyond the canopy. No footbridge existed until the Southern Railway electrification to Maidstone in 1939. *Lens of Sutton*

Below:
A general view of Bearsted station c1910 looking towards Hollingbourne. All six stations on this line, opened in 1884, had virtually identical structures for station buildings, waiting sheds, goods warehouses and signalboxes. The resemblance of the Saxby & Farmer signalbox to the LNWR standard design is clearly seen.
Lens of Sutton

Above left:
The same station in 1950. The only changes over the intervening years are the use of standard SR concrete components for platform facings and fencing, and the fitting of upper quadrant arms to the signal posts. *LGRP, courtesy David & Charles*

Left:
The exterior of Hollingbourne on 19 April 1981. The most noticeable modification is the replacement of slates with a corrugated asbestos roof covering.

Bottom left:
Lenham c1960 looking towards Charing. The brickwork here is red rather than the yellow stock used elsewhere on the line. *Lens of Sutton*

Above and Below:
The station at Charing, built in red brick rather than the white of those nearer Maidstone, has changed very little since it was built.

10 Individual Designs

Although LCDR stations were more standardised than those of most companies there were, nevertheless, a number of unique structures.

One of the most outstanding was Queenborough, built by the independent Sittingbourne & Sheerness Railway in 1860. Use of highly exaggerated gables and steep roof pitches, usually associated with ecclesiastical architecture, gave the station a singular appearance. The proportions of the building were, on the whole, nightmarish, giving the gimcrack look of a tin tabernacle.

A feature used at Queenborough was twin round headed windows surmounted by a single, large brick arch set into a wall, a device also used at the line's terminus at Sheerness Dockyard.

Less spectacular, but still quaint, was the small station at Newington, opened in 1862, where a hipped roof pavilion was flanked by two gabled wings with a projecting porch on the road side, perfectly set off by two miniature awnings, complete with valancing. The station looked like a toy or a caricature. Also in 1862 Shoreham, on the Sevenoaks, Maidstone & Tunbridge Railway, had a small brick gabled structure built, totally unlike anything else on the line.

In 1882 Otford received a plain brick station in a style not dissimilar to stations of 20 years earlier but rather more cheerful in that it was built of red brick. Such conservatism is not really surprising on the LCDR; its wagon designs remained unchanged, other than in detail, throughout the railway's separate existence.

Timber was a material rarely favoured by the LCDR, in direct contrast to its rival. At Selling what amounted to a timber version of the Farningham Road type of station was put up in 1860; the living accommodation was subsequently rebuilt. A generally similar but smaller building went up the following year at Meopham with a brick house adjacent but not attached. Much later, in 1871, Westgate-on-Sea had a rather more elaborate structure with diagonal planking and valancing under the eaves on the road side, rather in the LBSCR manner. An SER influence was evident at Sheerness-on-Sea where a plain hipped roof building of undistinguished appearance was put up in 1883.

The Gravesend West Street branch, which opened in 1886, had each of its stations built to an individual design. Rosherville, which served the nearby Gardens, a favourite spot for outings towards the end of Victoria's reign, comprised a single island platform with a canopy, access being by a covered footbridge because the station was located in a cutting. Southfleet had a similar platform arrangement but with a long single storey building under a steeply pitched hipped roof. The terminus at Gravesend had a large, brick building set in the vee where the line to the pier deviated. The accommodation provided was commodious, if singularly unattractive.

Below:
Queenborough's building was certainly extraordinary. A mass of gables – most of which seemed strangely out of proportion to the size of the windows – its bulk is well shown in this c1908 picture. Iron signs advertising products as diverse as Pears Soap, BDV Cigarettes, Shepherd Neame Ales and Sanitas disinfectants cling to every available foot of wall. At this stage Queenborough was the junction for the Sheppey Light Railway, whose bay is in the foreground. The SER goods brake in the foregound, SECR No 387, is the brake employed on the branch. *Lens of Sutton*

Above:
Another view of Queenborough with two sailors reminding one of the strong Naval presence in Sheppey. Slightly earlier in date than the previous picture, the station building still retains a lamp over the entrance that would not have looked out of place outside a gin palace. The massive weighing machine with handrails is of interest. *Courtesy K. Marx*

Below:
The road approach side of Queenborough looks equally bizarre with two pairs of small windows on the ground floor each surmounted by a large arch in contrasting brickwork. The entrance where the arch is partly filled by a diagonally boarded wooden screen adds to the already peculiar appearance. An ex LCDR six-wheel brake with central guards compartment, known as a 'camel back', is in the background. *Lens of Sutton*

Above:
A terminus at Sheerness Dockyard was built in the same strange style as Queenborough. Closed to passengers in 1922, it remained open for goods until the late 1960s, albeit in a derelict state. *J. L. Smith*

Below:
Otford, a late one-off design of 1892, was in shape a reversion to the austere early style, lacking all the Gothic touches of many stations put up in the 1880s. The warm red brick however helped its appearance considerably. Photographed in 1976.

Right:
Two views of Selling. The general view looking towards Canterbury shows the timber goods shed, put up at the same time as the station buildings in 1860. The waiting shed too is original. The second view shows that the station building was a timber version of the style used at Adisham and Farningham Road. Beyond it is the 1901 stationmaster's house. *Lens of Sutton*

THE STATION, SELLING.

73

Top:
Newington had a curious small brick building on the up platform with an LCDR design signalbox of the late 1870s next to it. The signalbox nameboard is a typical LCDR fitting in its use of the word 'box' without the qualifying 'signal'. The waiting shed is contemporary with the station. *Lens of Sutton*

Above:
The small and quite undistinguished red brick station at Shoreham, as photographed on 23 April 1984.

Right:
Southfleet, looking towards Gravesend in 1922. Together with the next station, Rosherville, it was the only example of a rural island platform station. The yard appears busy in this view. The long building with its hipped slate roof was unlike anything else on the system. *H. J. Patterson Rutherford*

The South Eastern & Chatham Railway

The simple brick building of 1902 at Fawkham that replaced one destroyed by fire two years previously. The gabled canopy gives a note of distinction to an otherwise very dull structure, and the LCDR waiting shed is much earlier and may well be the original. All the buildings were replaced by CLASP structures c1969. *Lens of Sutton*

11 Stations

Reconstruction of country stations under the hand of the Management Committee was limited to some three examples, plus a junction station for the new Bexhill branch at Crowhurst.

Crowhurst Junction was a large station intended almost entirely as an interchange for the Bexhill line, as it was situated some way from any centre of population. Facilities provided were generous with four roads through the station, long platforms and awnings of considerable width. The buildings were similar to those constructed in connection with the widening of the line at Chislehurst at about the same time, and were direct descendents of Walmer (1881). Indeed, they were hardly an advance on those at North Camp of the 1860s and appeared curiously dated.

Fawkham station burnt down in 1900 and was replaced in 1902 by a plain brick station which did have one distinguishing feature – charming ridge and furrow awnings on both forecourt and platform sides. The design was not repeated and the station was demolished circa 1969.

Merstham was rebuilt in 1905 with a small building which showed the impact of Edwardian villa influences. External wall treatment comprised brick lower parts with rough cast above complemented by brick decoration. Windows were casements, and the eaves, with a pediment above the entrance, displayed a movement towards the neo-Georgian style then very much in vogue. It was in its modest way a 20th century building in the way that Crowhurst Junction was of the 19th century. Only the usual SER pattern awnings on the platform side detracted from its modernity.

Below:
Junction for the newly opened Bexhill branch, Crowhurst had an enormous station serving a small local community. Neat buildings were provided but, as this photograph taken not long after opening shows, they were rather dated. There is little progress made from the North Camp station buildings of the 1860s.
Lens of Sutton

Bottom:
Merstham's most attractive neo-Georgian station of 1905, photographed in 1907, is so different in spirit it is difficult to believe it is only three years later than Crowhurst. Pebbledash with red brick trim gives a bright, modern appearance. *Photomatic*

The next reconstruction, of Blackwater in 1910, took the form of a modernised version of the 1880s domestic revival of Nutley & Sandling Junction. The basic shape with half hipped roof (though at a lower pitch) was retained but simplified with the exclusion of the timber framing. Gone too was the gabled porch, to be replaced by a massive semi-circular pediment bearing the date of construction. Below this were large windows lighting the booking office. The most unusual feature of the design was the chimneys which were shaped brick with a simple concrete cap. The use of these simple forms, purged of any conventional decorative treatment and stripped of historical allusions, made this simple building a pioneer of the modern International style, and gave it an appearance of being constructed in the 1930s rather than 20 years earlier. It is unfortunate that an incongruous standard SER canopy was fitted and, even more so, that the station was demolished circa 1970.

Demolished at the same time was the 1914 building at Godstone, the third SECR rebuild, but it cannot be said to have rivalled the other two in interest. The architect had the problem of a difficult location; the platforms were at a higher level than the approach and so the building was two storeyed on the road side. It was a plain brick building with the usual canopy, but a pantiled roof was a unique use of the material on the SECR.

In complete contrast to the foregoing stations were the rudimentary structures on the Sheppey Light Railway opened in 1901. While some railways were light in name only, the Sheppey line had all the hallmarks of one: short timber platforms, small huts serving as halts and unprepossessing corrugated iron shacks at the larger stations. The style of the latter was indeed very close to that of stations on the Colonel Stephens' lines, right down to the sturdy posts with diagonal bracing at the top used to support the canopies. They seemed most appropriate to the flat wilderness that comprised much of the Isle of Sheppey.

In common with most railways in the 10 years preceding the Great War, the SECR opened a number of halts. They had the timber platforms and simple post and rail fencing with oil lamps attached to wooden posts that are associated with the word 'halt', but the neat timber buildings were a definite improvement on the LBSCR's corrugated iron shelters.

Below:
The new station at Blackwater nears completion in 1910. The old gentlemen's toilet and the roader shed contrast strangely with the modernity of the new building. The canopy looks a little like an afterthought and the mid-Victorian pattern brackets are very much at odds with the clean, unfussy style of the remainder of the structure. *Lens of Sutton*

Above:
East Malling Halt, opened in 1913, was very similar to Leigh with an office for the ticket clerk and a waiting shelter combined and oil lamps on top of short wooden posts. *Lens of Sutton*

Below:
The Sheppey Light Railway meandered across the meadows of the island and its installations were in the best light railway tradition. Eastchurch here looks like part of the Colonel Stephens' empire with its typical iron building with canopy resting on triangular based supports. An 'RI' draws in with one of the push pull sets converted from SECR steam rail motors. It looks as though nobody has sat on the platform seat for years. *Real Photographs*

12 Waiting Sheds

Waiting sheds are, by their nature, somewhat ephemeral structures, and their early history on the SER is shrouded in mystery. They were liable to frequent replacement and alteration and were not always the subject of drawings. Dating is consequently difficult. While standard designs did evolve in the 1880s, the early shelters were frequently one-off designs, varying in both size and style. An early shelter at Penshurst had a rounded roof, but the great majority had monopitched roofs extended at the front to form a small canopy. Several had vertical planking and these seem to have been the most numerous type to survive into recent years. Some examples were those at Grove Ferry, Chilham, Sturry and Smeeth. A very plain variety was erected at Staplehurst and Pluckley (the latter still exists). Marden, drawn here, was an interesting variant of 1876 with diagonal boarding.

Two standard designs appeared. One, the most common, was very distinctive with paired windows on the front and sides. Horizontal clapboarding was applied to the exterior of the wooden frame, and groove and tongue vertical boarding to the inside. The rafters were supported by two large beams which formed the top of the frame and which were rather elegantly shaped at the ends.

The other design was similar in constructional details but differed in having a single sash window in place of the fixed paired lights. Some shelters had windows at the ends; some did not. Standard valancing was fitted to some of the shelters but this was almost certainly an addition in SECR days; none would appear to have been built with valancing. Examples of both types were legion; of the first type Frant, Higham, Chilworth and Cuxton may be mentioned; of the second type Maidstone Barracks, Lydd and Wateringbury. Again precise dates for some of the shelters are sketchy, but most were put up in the 1880s.

A development of the type were the shelters on the Bexleyheath Railway, opened in 1895. These retained the paired windows but the monopitched roof was replaced by one gently sloping from front to rear. A similar shelter was erected at Whitstable Harbour. The final type was the larger shelter taking the form of a section of awning, matching that of the main station building, with screen walls to the rear and sides. Some, such as Dunton Green and Hildenborough, had straight edges to the top of the valancing, while Knockholt and Hythe had curved tops matching their respective station buildings.

Early LCDR shelters were small with vertical groove and tongue boarding. Roofs were not nearly as steeply pitched as those of the SER shelters and in some cases were almost flat. A shallow canopy projected at the front and all LCDR shelters had a simple form of valancing. Windows had fixed sashes. Examples of these early shelters were at Teynham, Sole Street and Shepherds Well. Sometimes the front of the shelter was left completely open as at Adisham.

The Sevenoaks line had larger shelters with an attractive valance design and a steeper roof pitch. Later shelters had horizontal boarding, steeply pitched roofs and the valancing extending the full width of the building as at Kearsney and Queensborough. Although there was a fair degree of standardisation, oddities inevitably arose – none more so than at Farningham Road where the base of the water tank was (and is) used as a shelter.

The extension to Maidstone saw some substantial shelters built. These had brick ends and rear, with the front of timber. They were very well lit by eight windows and, unusually, had doors to keep them draught free. Perhaps to compensate for this relative luxury, there was no canopy on the front as was usually the case. An even more distinctive design was evolved for the section of the line from Maidstone to Ashford. Brick shelters, designed to complement the rather ponderous station buildings on this stretch of line, and sharing the same pointed windows, iron pillars and deep valance, were put up. All were open at the front although Charing was later filled in with timber.

Below:
An early waiting shed of non-standard design at Pluckley, photographed on 3 June 1984. A very similar structure was also located at Staplehurst. The wide non-opening windows are distinctive, as are the generally box like proportions of the shelter.

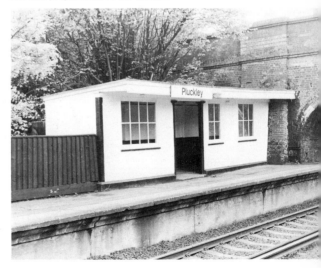

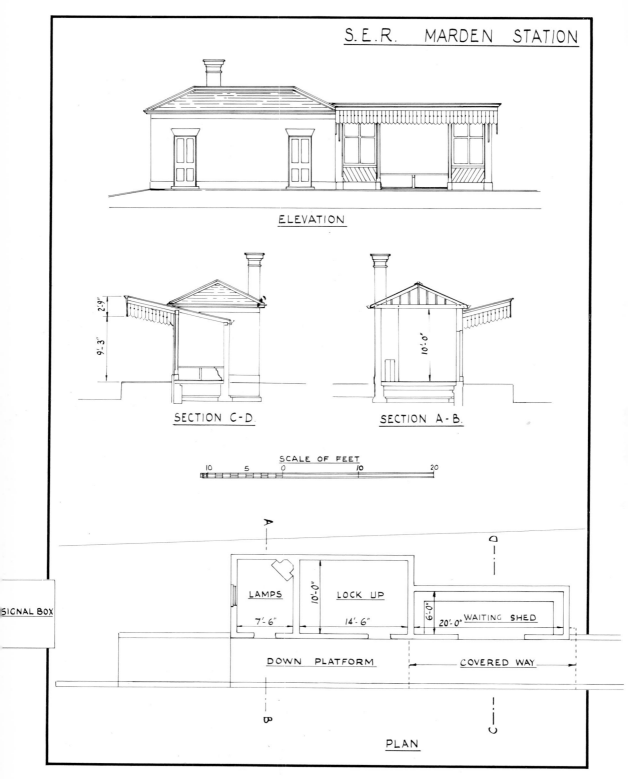

S.E.R. MARDEN STATION

ELEVATION

SECTION C-D.

SECTION A-B.

SCALE OF FEET

10   5   0   10   20

SIGNAL BOX

LAMPS
7'-6"

LOCK UP
14'-6"
10'-0"

WAITING SHED
6'-0"
20'-0"

DOWN PLATFORM

COVERED WAY

PLAN

2'-9"
9'-3"
10'-0"

Left:
Marden lamp room, lock up and waiting shed as existing in 1890. The canopy to the shelter appears to have been modified between construction in 1876 and a photograph taken in 1890. *Drawing by W. E. Rowley*

Top:
Marden in 1890, looking towards Tonbridge, showing the waiting shed and lamp room of 1876 as shown in the accompanying drawing. *Lens of Sutton*

Above:
One of the standard SER shelters with paired windows, in rather decrepit state, at Betchworth in the 1960s.
Ian Allan Library

Right:
A similar shelter at Cuxton was fitted with valancing in late SECR days. Photographed 23 April 1984.

Above left:
Selling has a fine example of an early LCDR waiting shed in original condition. The box-like appearance is considerably improved by the attractive valancing on the awning. Photographed 22 September 1975. *J. Scrace*

Left:
A representative example, built in 1887, of the other standard type of SER waiting shed at **Ore** in 1970. This picture clearly shows the wide beam with attractively curved ends supporting the rafters which was characteristic of this type of shed.

Above:
An elongated version of the standard shelter was provided at **Sole Street**. It has now lost the lower part of its valancing and the sashes have been removed from the windows. Photographed 23 April 1984.

Above right:
The waiting shelter at **Adisham** is an open fronted varient of the LCDR design, dating back to the opening of the station in 1861; the valancing has been trimmed. Photographed 3 June 1984.

Right:
Shoreham's waiting shelter was enlivened by an intricate valance. Photographed 2 April 1970, the structure has since been replaced. *J. Scrace*

Left:
The unique shelter at Farningham Road which was formerly the base of a water tank. Photographed 23 April 1984.

Below:
Borough Green & Wrotham waiting shed. A similar structure was erected at West Malling, and both dated back to the rebuilding of the two stations in 1880. They were highly distinctive in being large, partly brick built and with no hint of the usual LCDR valance. Photographed 23 April 1984.

Right:
Harrietsham is a typical shed on the Maidstone–Ashford line with brickwork, windows and heavy valancing to match the main station. Photographed 19 April 1981.

Below right:
The ivy clad shelter at Charing, the only one of this pattern to have the front filled in, as photographed on 3 June 1984.

13 Signalboxes

The earliest pattern of signalboxes to be found on the South Eastern were, like those on many rural lines of the 1860s, small huts at ground level, usually placed at the end of the platform ramp by the crossing between the staggered platforms. These huts were of distinctive appearance, having a gable facing the track and a group of three sash windows on each side. These structures began to be superseded in the 1870s, a process which seems to have been completed in the early 1890s. However, many of the huts remained in use for a variety of purposes forming additional station accommodation.

There were some curious early signalboxes of a larger size. On the main line near Folkestone a timber box with raised beading was built, while its roof was for all practical purposes like a canopy as employed on many SER stations such as Knockholt – with a gentle curve and valancing. Another box at Gomshall Crossing had the usual clapboard sides and sash windows but combined with a flat roof.

In the early 1870s the nearest thing that the SER had to a standard signalbox was developed. It continued to be built well into the 20th century. In an age when most companies had very individualistic designs, the SER had one of the most distinctive. Usually built of timber throughout, but occasionally having a base of brick, its most unusual feature was the use of standard constructional techniques and fittings common to the contemporary station buildings. Thus, while the walls had clapboard siding, the windows were sashes mounted within the walls. This was quite at variance with the usual British practice where large window frames, specifically designed for signalboxes, ran the entire length of the front and part of the sides. The size and grouping of the windows varied considerably to the point where almost every box of this type was different.

Simultaneously with the SER's own design of box, from the 1880s, signalboxes were built to various contractors' designs. The most common and perhaps the most standardised boxes to be erected were those constructed by Messrs Saxby & Farmer between 1892 and 1894. The great majority of these boxes were of wood on a brick base (one at least, Boxhill, was all timber) and had deep eaves which, coupled with the lack of bargeboards, gave them a relatively modern appearance.

Stevens & Co built a small number of boxes, notably those on the Westerham and Hayes branches in 1881 and 1882, to its own design, a style more often associated with the London, Chatham & Dover Railway. McKenzie & Holland built some attractive boxes with bargeboards on the Hawkhurst branch and the Bexleyheath Railway. Some large and imposing gabled boxes, also with bargeboards, were put up by the Railway Signal Co circa 1893. The Dutton & Co boxes of 1893 at Wadhurst and Blackwater appear to have been unique on the SER. Why Dutton was chosen for the Wadhurst installation, when the remainder of the 1893 re-signalling on the Hastings line was carried out by Saxby & Farmer, remains a mystery.

There was less variety on the London, Chatham & Dover Railway. The company evolved its own box design in the 1870s, and this took the form of a gable ended structure, distinguished by vertical planking and a very gentle curve to each of the window frames. Besides Adisham of 1878, drawn here, examples included Newington and Sevenoaks Bat and Ball.

A great many boxes were built by Stevens & Co to a design that appeared a little old fashioned by the 1880s when many of them were built. Again they had vertical timbering, but a valance over the end windows and generally a rather squat appearance set them apart from the company built boxes.

Saxby & Farmer contributed many of its distinctive top-light pattern hipped roof boxes of the type first seen on the LBSCR in 1876. The LCDR examples were generally a little later than those on the Brighton line and tended to be of either all timber construction or of timber on a brick base.

This design was adapted by the LCDR for its own construction in succession to the gabled boxes, and examples continued to be built into the 20th century. The brackets provide the only clear way of distinguishing between the Saxby & Farmer and LCDR built boxes, while the later examples had top-lights with square rather than semi-circular corners.

The new line between Maidstone and Ashford opened in 1884, had Saxby & Farmer gabled boxes, quite unlike anything else on the system and resembling to some extent the standard designs of the LNWR.

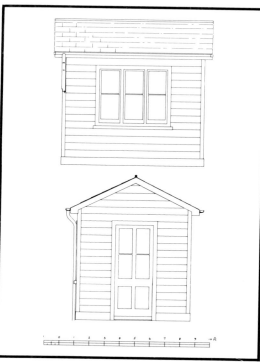

Above left:
A Stevens & Co signalbox, Birchington-on-Sea. One of
many such signalboxes on the LCDR constructed in the
1870s and 80s, they were all somewhat antiquated in
appearance. Photographed 10 September 1968.
J. Scrace

Left:
Shepherds Well signalbox was probably built in 1878,
the same year as the Adisham box. Like Adisham, it is a
gable ended box with vertical planking constructed by
the LCDR itself rather than by contractors. Three of the
sashes at the front retain the curved top to the windows,
while the others visible have been replaced.

Above:
West Malling was of Saxby & Farmer design and was
built in 1881. Photographed 23 April 1984.

Right:
One of the distinctive Saxby & Farmer boxes built in
1884 for the Maidstone–Ashford line at Charing stands
awaiting its inevitable fate after closure in April 1984.
The lever frame has already been removed.

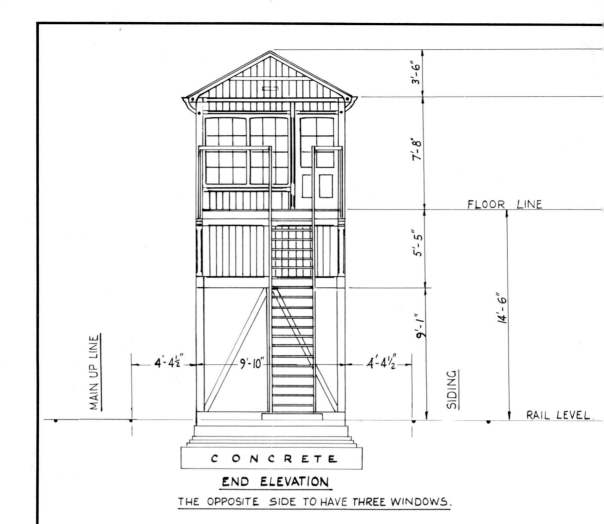

3'-6"

7'-8"

FLOOR LINE

5'-5"

MAIN UP LINE

4'-4½"   9'-10"   4'-4½"

9'-1"

14'-6"

SIDING

RAIL LEVEL

C O N C R E T E

END ELEVATION

THE OPPOSITE SIDE TO HAVE THREE WINDOWS.

L. C. & D. RY.

ADISHAM STATION

SIGNAL BOX

Adisham signalbox as built in 1878. It was a tall
example of the LCDR's own design of signalbox; The
timber framing of the lower part was later covered with
vertical boarding. *Drawing by W. E. Rowley*

Scale: 4mm/1 ft.

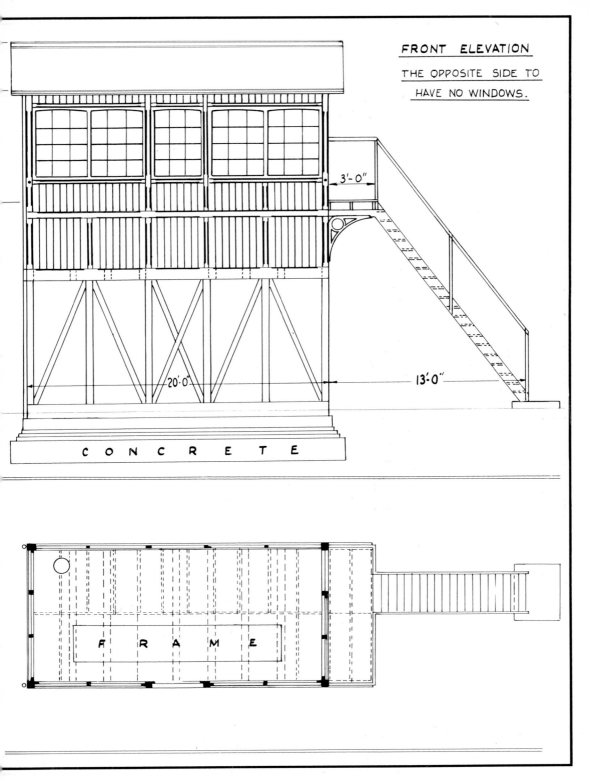

FRONT ELEVATION

THE OPPOSITE SIDE TO
HAVE NO WINDOWS.

3'-0"

13'-0"

20'-0"

CONCRETE

FRAME

14 Goods Warehouses

Perhaps not surprisingly, in view of the much greater timespan involved in their construction, the goods warehouses of the SER were much more variegated in appearance than those of its neighbours.

The earliest structures were small gabled brick sheds such as formerly existed at Marden, Headcorn and Penshurst. There were numerous variations on this theme; Chilham (1861) had recessed panels, Shalford and Wokingham were large examples. Some very distinctive designs complemented the attractive Tress stations on the Hastings line of 1881. Warehouses at Wadhurst, Ticehurst Road, Etchingham, Roberts-bridge and Battle were built to a common style, with a roof pitched quite steeply and very narrow windows in the side panels. A similar one was erected at Appledore.

Perhaps the most interesting warehouses were a number built in 1856 at Northfleet, Gravesend, Snodland and Aylesford, and the latter two still exist. Built in a far more ornate style than was generally the case, they had hipped roofs with dentilled brickwork below, semi-circular door openings and blind arches on the side, and attractive cast iron window frames with rounded tops. The impression of careful detailing was reinforced by the excellent treatment of the chimneys at the ends, these being paired. These warehouses were comparatively large; Snodland formed the rear screen of a platform canopy, a device also used at Appledore.

Smaller warehouses were built the same year at Yalding, Wateringbury and East Farleigh. These were distinguished by semi-circular iron windows, semi-circular door openings (though to a much less extreme arc than those of the LCDR) and stone facings at the gable edges, a feature repeated many times in other goods sheds.

There were many other variations. Westenhanger had a small brick shed mounted beside the line rather than spanning it: access was via a large side door. A handsome early range of two storey warehouses with gables facing the track still stand in Staplehurst goods yard. Intended for agricultural traffic, they have sliding doors out of which goods could be loaded directly into wagons. Similar structures once stood at Tonbridge and Ashford but were demolished many years ago. Westerham, opened 1881, had a gabled all-wood shed. Frequently used in later years were lock-up goods sheds, known to the SER as 'roader sheds', mounted on station platforms which would be used for sundries or when the level of traffic did not justify a full size structure. They were constructed of wood and usually had the gable end facing the platform above double doors. Examples of this type were legion, some being Dunton Green, Hildenborough and Wadhurst. Less common was a variation with the gables away from the track, such as the shed at Sandgate.

As might be expected from the severity of its stations, the goods warehouses put up by the LCDR tended to be plain, unadorned structures, and designs did not vary greatly throughout the company's existence. The great majority of the warehouses were built of brick, generally with gable ended roofs; most had semi-circular ventilators at the ends while a most distinctive feature was the end doors which were rounded to fit the openings. The area at the side of the warehouses where goods were loaded from the platforms on to the drays was usually covered with a substantial awning extending the length of the building.

The smaller warehouses such as those at Teynham and Rainham were generally of three bays in length; The larger examples could be up to six bays. Over the years, goods offices were frequently added at the front or rear. Skylights were normally provided to light the interior of the structures, and windows were sometimes placed in the recessed panels of some of the later sheds, for example Eynsford.

There were a number of exceptions to the usual pattern of things. Selling had a timber goods shed to match its timber station, the warehouse bearing a family resemblance to the early brick examples. On the Maidstone–Ashford line the rounded brick arch over the doors was replaced by a rolled steel joist, a window was fitted at the ends in place of the louvred ventilators, and the side awning extended only over the doors, not the full length of the building.

Above right:
Two views of the early group of agricultural warehouses at Staplehurst, photographed on 3 June 1984. Comparison with the photograph of 1887 in Chapter 1 reveals a few alterations over the years. One set of sliding doors has been bricked up as has one of the doors to the left. The warehouses still bear the name of a company now well known in the railway modelling field.

Right:
A substantial warehouse at Reigate, probably dating from the opening of the line in 1849. A workmanlike structure of unadorned appearance, it nevertheless has extended battens which, with their curved ends, form a pattern on the fascia board. Photographed 1982.

Far right:
The small goods warehouse at Westenhanger has had its appearance somewhat transformed since the photographs in Chapter 5 were taken, by the removal of the parapet walls of the gables at each end. Goods would be taken straight out of wagons on a siding (which has since been removed), through the large opening at the side and transferred to a cart which would be taken out through the double doors at the end. Photographed 3 June 1984.

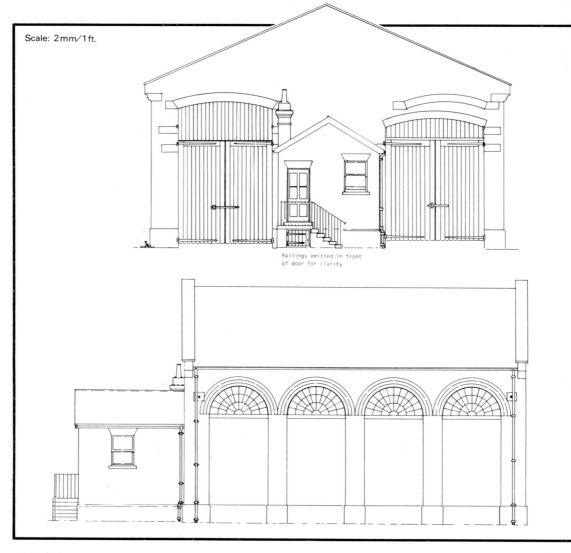

Scale: 2mm/1ft.

Railings omitted in front
of door for clarity

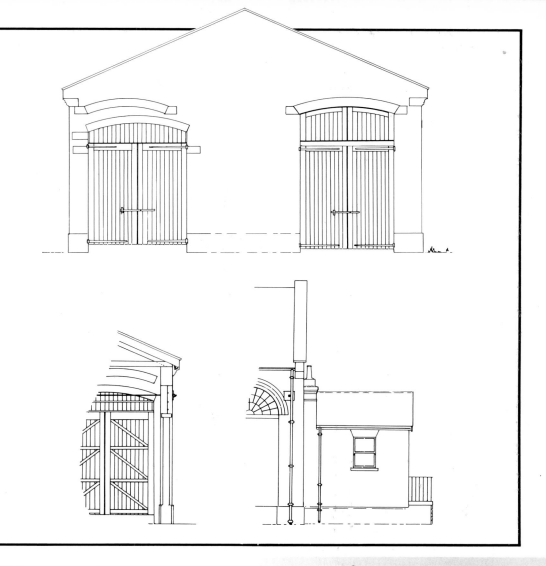

Left:
The 1851 warehouse at Robertsbridge, photographed on 15 April 1984 and unaltered since construction. The large side doors are at variance with the usual SER practice of end doors for access by road.

Right:
The similar shed at Battle, photographed from the opposite side. The slit like windows were a distinctive feature of the design. Battle, like several of the other warehouses of this pattern was later fitted with a separate goods office, in 1861 in this particular case. Photographed 15 April 1984.

Above:
Wateringbury goods warehouse. The drawing, with measurements derived in the main from brick counting. depicts the building in its present form.
Drawing by C. J. Perkins

Left:
Two views of Wateringbury goods shed. The large
semi-circular windows of this style are particularly
attractive. The doorway on the railway side of the
building has had its arch rebuilt, the brickwork of the
former arch being clearly visible. The goods office at the
end is a later addition of 1900. Photographed 19 April
1981.

Below:
The large and imposing warehouse of 1856 at Snodland
has suffered minor alterations to fit it for its present role.
The large side door has been bricked up and one of
those at the end modified also, the fine chimneys have
been removed. Photographed 23 April 1984.

Right:
A detail view of the chimneys of the now demolished
Gravesend warehouse gives a good indication of their
appearance. Photographed 10 April 1969.   *A. M. Riley*

Bottom:
The similar structure at Aylesford on 19 April 1981. As
in the case of Snodland, numerous modifications to
doors and windows have been made.

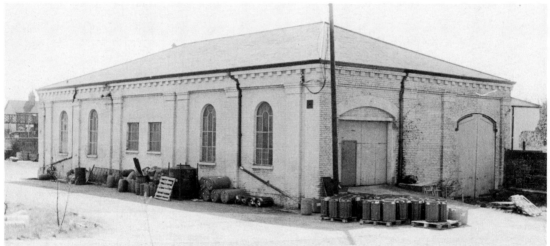

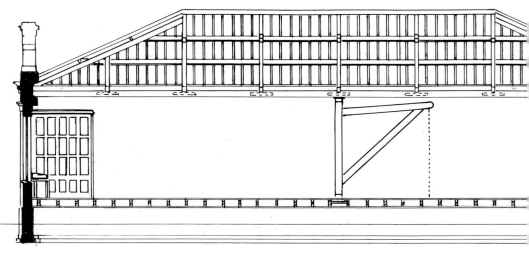

SECTION ON LINE C.D.

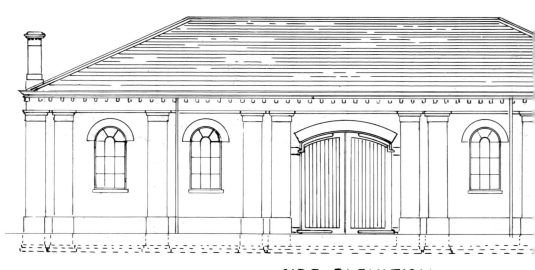

SIDE ELEVATION.

Snodland goods warehouse as designed. It is not known whether it ever received the decorative scrolls on the chimneys – other sheds of this type certainly did but there is no photographic evidence that Snodland was amongst them. *Drawing by W. E. Rowley*

Scale: 2mm/1ft.

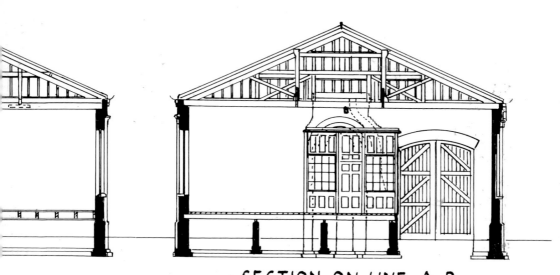

SECTION ON LINE A.B

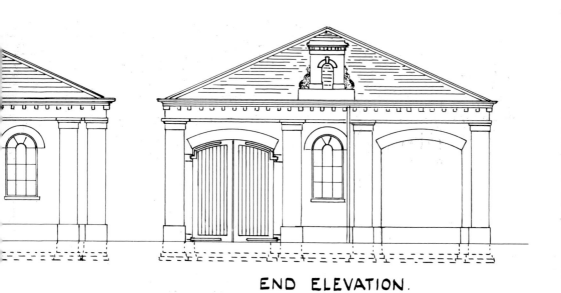

END ELEVATION.

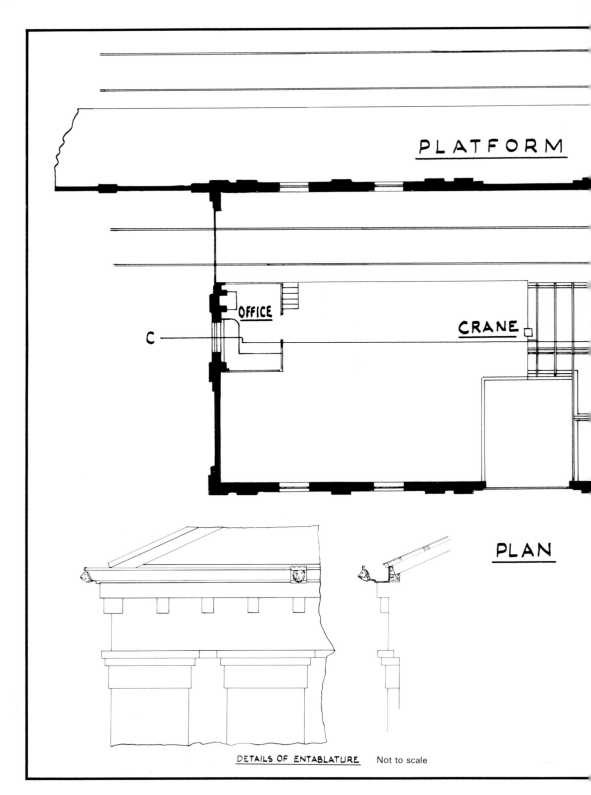

PLATFORM

OFFICE

C

CRANE

PLAN

DETAILS OF ENTABLATURE   Not to scale

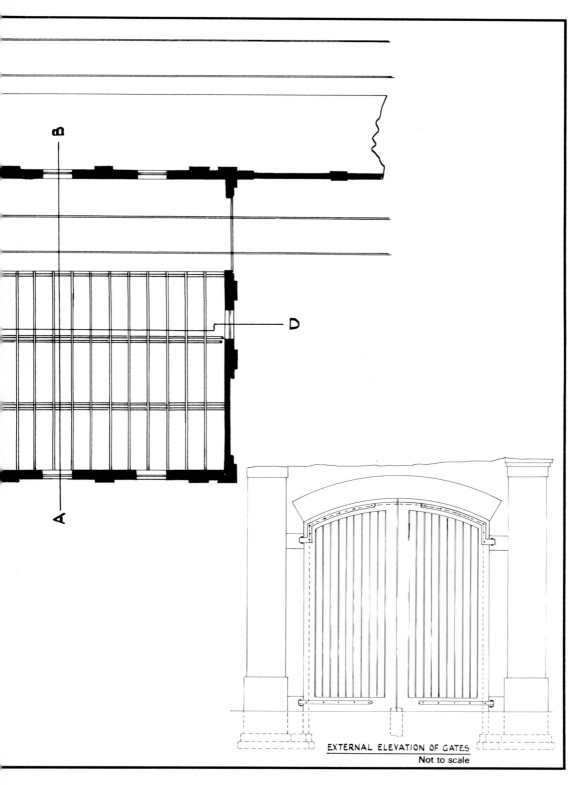

B

D

A

EXTERNAL ELEVATION OF GATES
Not to scale

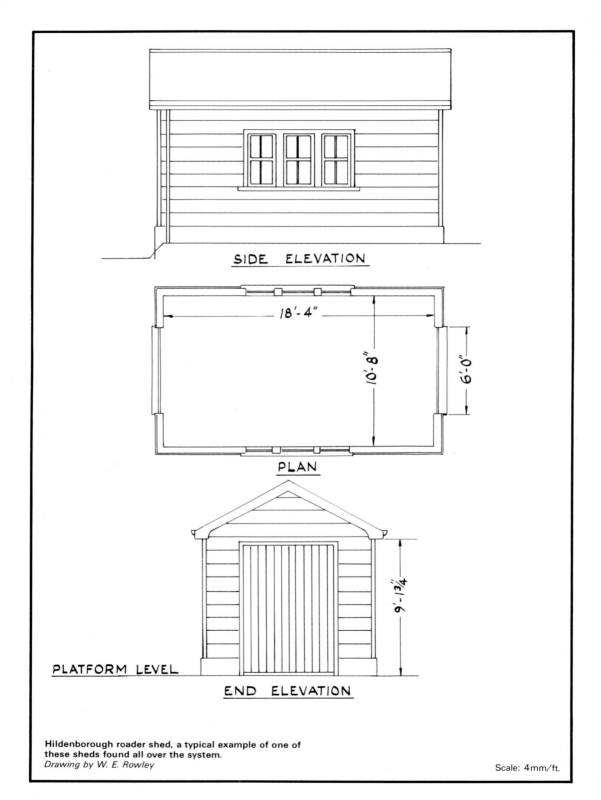

SIDE ELEVATION

18'-4"

10'-8"

6'-0"

PLAN

9'-1¾"

PLATFORM LEVEL

END ELEVATION

Hildenborough roader shed, a typical example of one of
these sheds found all over the system.
Drawing by W. E. Rowley

Scale: 4mm/ft.

Top:
Kearsney is a fine example of an early LCDR goods warehouse. The distinctive round arch to the doorway, and circular ventilator, present in the great majority of LCDR warehouses, are clearly visible. The dentilled brickwork at the top of the recesses in the side is also fairly common. The rear view shows the two recessed panels (the track did not run right through the building in some of the early warehouses) and the one major alteration in recent years – the removal of the canopy over the two sets of doors. Photographed 3 June 1984.

Above:
Built to the same drawing as the warehouse at Rainham in 1861 was that at Adisham, now part of a small factory. It lacks the dentilled brickwork of Kearsney and has blind arches rather than flat topped recessed panels at the rear. Otherwise, it is very similar. Photographed 3 June 1984.

Right:
The small warehouse at Shoreham was built in 1862 and still retains its canopy on the road side. It lacks the rounded arches at the ends and the ventilators of other LCDR warehouses. Photographed 23 April 1984.

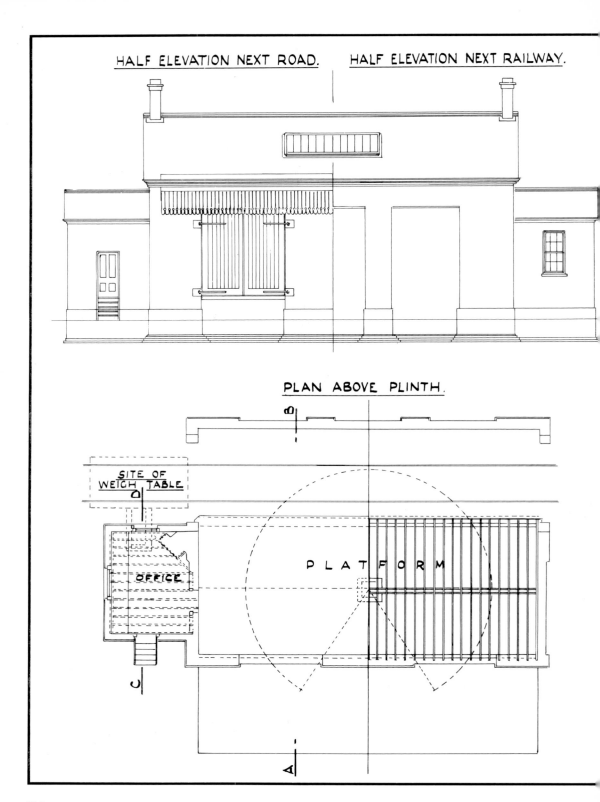

HALF ELEVATION NEXT ROAD.   HALF ELEVATION NEXT RAILWAY.

PLAN ABOVE PLINTH.

SITE OF
WEIGH TABLE

OFFICE

P L A T F O R M

END ELEVATION.

LEVEL OF RAILS.

SECTION A.B.

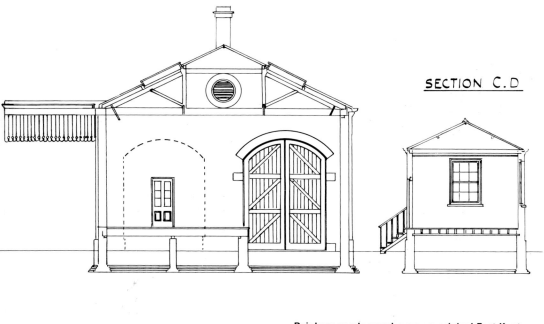

SECTION C.D

Rainham goods warehouse, an original East Kent Railway structure. The warehouses at Adisham and Kearsney shared the same dimensions but did not have the track running through the shed. Kearsney also had differences in the brickwork. *Drawing by W. E. Rowley*

0   5   10   15   20   25   30

15 Ancillary Structures

The country goods yard provided a natural centre for local industry and a convenient location for builders' merchants, grain stores and hop dealers. An interesting assortment of buildings grew up, some quite substantial, others ephemeral. Old carriage and wagon bodies were much favoured and many of the shacks had a homegrown appearance. As goods yards have disappeared under tarmac to provide car parks or have had housing or factories built over them, the mortality rate amongst such structures is high, far greater than that of station buildings or warehouses. Unfortunately, they seem rarely to have attracted the attention of photographers.

Nevertheless, it is possible to illustrate some interesting survivals. The two warehouses at Battle and Marden are representative of what seems to have been a common arrangement whereby materials brought in by rail to the upper storey of the building could be lowered on to carts at the lower level, and vice versa. The Marden warehouse, since demolished, was a typically Kentish clapboarded structure, while Battle was in yellow stock brick. Marden was most likely used for hop traffic.

The most unusual survival of all is to be found at Farningham Road where a coal merchant still uses an ex-LCDR third of circa 1880 as a store. Considering its age it is in quite good condition.

To move on to railway owned structures, larger country stations often had stables in the goods yard. Again, these have largely disappeared but those at Aldershot North Camp, built in 1866, were still being used for their original purpose in 1983. This was a particularly large structure due to the extensive military traffic at the station.

Both the SER and LCDR had their own distinctive practices in platform fittings and furniture. For platform fencing the SER favoured vertical close boarding, with post and rail as another popular option. The LCDR preferred iron railings and brick walling.

The SER emblazoned the company's initials on the end of its platform seats; the LCDR was more circumspect, its seats being small benches with distinctive cast iron frames. Lamps were another area of difference between the two companies: although there was no rigid standardisation, the SER's tended to be what may best be described as the 'barleysugar twist' variety, rather like those of the LSWR, while the LCDR favoured a fluted pattern.

Accommodation was often provided in those cases where a flat was not incorporated in the station building. A substantial detached house would be provided for the stationmaster with a row of cottages for other staff. These were usually built to a standard design. Identical rows of cottages built in the Tudor manner with diapered brickwork on the gable end may still be seen at Staplehurst, Pluckley and Westenhanger. They were attractive but very small.

Right:
Agricultural warehouse at Marden. Not, it is believed, an SER designed structure but an interesting example of the vernacular building to be found in many country goods yards. Drawn from photographs, some details are conjectural. *Drawing by C. J. Perkins*

Below:
Goudhurst on the Hawkhurst branch c1905. This charming picture is the very epitome of the rural Kentish railway scene. On the right stands a group of oasthouses while someone has casually left their bicycle lying on the verge. A corner of the goods yard is to the left. In it stands an ancient SER brake van which has lost most of its paint probably used as a store. The station building is just out of sight but the signalbox is visible behind the prominent sign of the Seaborne Coal & Coke Co which was 'also at Paddock Wood and Yalding'. Some of the latter company's stock in trade is probably in the back of the cart waiting in the road by the level crossing.
G. L. Gundry collection

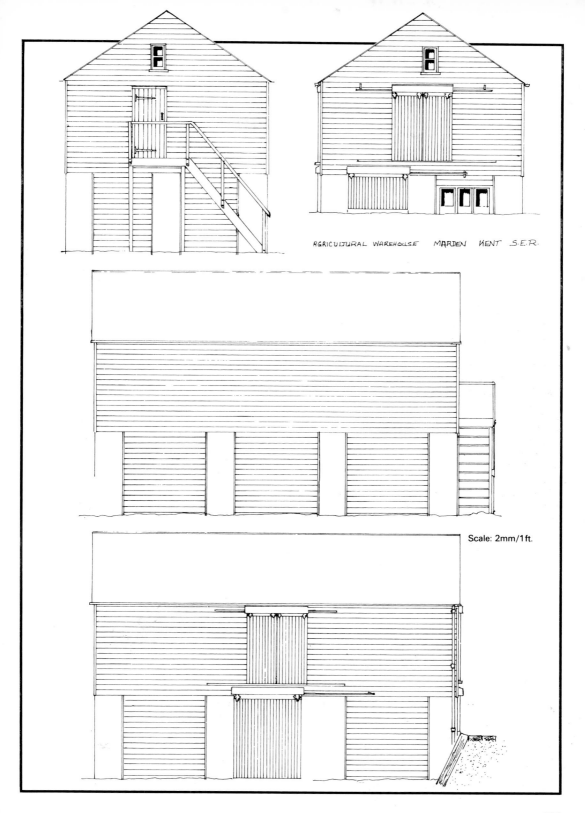

AGRICULTURAL WAREHOUSE   MARDEN   KENT S.E.R.

Scale: 2mm/1ft.

107

Above left:
A split level store in yellow brick at Battle. Access is gained at rail level via the loading platform and at road level by a door at the side. Photographed 15 April 1984.

Far left:
A clapboarded agricultural warehouse at Marden built on the same principle and photographed in the 1960s when nearing the end of its days. Such structures were once commonplace in country goods yards. *C. J. Perkins*

Left:
Redundant signalboxes on the SER often found new uses. This early box at Marden is doing duty as a hut in a corner of the coal yard. *C. J. Perkins*

Far below left:
The SECR made great use of iron railings and gates in its goods yards after 1899, and the boss prominently displaying the company's initials as in this example at Staplehurst was frequently found. Photographed 3 June 1984.

Below left:
Once country goods yards were full of relics like this coal office at Farningham Road. Now, such sights are rare indeed and this ex-LCDR four wheel Third body of c1880 is a remarkable survivor. It has spent far longer here than it did in service. Photographed 23 April 1984.

Top:
A sizeable block of stables at Aldershot North Camp. They were built in 1866 and were still being used for their intended purpose when photographed on 24 April 1983.

Above right:
A South Eastern Railway seat at Dorking on 1 February 1969 complete with the company's initials. The SECR perpetuated the design (though without the initials) and it is still a common sight. *D. Clayton*

Right:
Quite different in appearance was the LCDR seat which had a cast frame. This one was photographed at West Malling on 23 April 1984.

Left:
Some of the last surviving oil lamps were those at Ham Street, here seen in 1974.

Below:
When the 1882 waiting shed in front of the goods warehouse at Kearsney was demolished recently, the station name painted on the wall was revealed. Photographed 3 June 1984.

Bottom:
Gomshall Lane Crossing in the 1930s. The pretty cottage dates from the opening of the line and is similar to one at the east end of Rye station. The level crossing gates are of the early vertical timbered pattern.
H. A. Vallance

Above:
A group of four cottages at Pluckley, very little altered externally. They differ from similar groups elsewhere on the main line in having two round arched lights to the windows on the ground floor, a feature they share with all the other cottages in Pluckley. The local landowner, Sir Edward Cholmeley Dering, considered they brought good luck and had them fitted to the cottages and other buildings on his estate. Photographed 3 June 1984.

Right:
The stationmaster at Pluckley had a most attractive detached house in the domestic revival style. It was probably built c1888 as it was very similar to one provided at Sandling Junction that year. Photographed 3 June 1984.

Below:
A rare use of stone in the construction of the crossing keeper's house at Appledore station, as photographed in 1974.

Above:
A pair of LCDR cottages at Bekesbourne. That on the right has received a bay window in recent years. The arrangement of two gables meeting at right angles was much favoured by railway companies, the LBSC and LSWR both building many examples. Photographed 3 June 1984.

Left:
The staff at Kearsney in May 1895. Signalman Gambell was, at only 4ft in height, apparently the shortest signalman on the LCDR. The stationmaster, Mr Curtis, is fourth from the left. The picture gives an idea of the numbers of staff then employed at a country station. It also provides a clear view of an LCDR station nameboard. *Southern Railway Magazine, courtesy A. M. Riley*

Below:
The end at Goudhurst. Lengths of track are being unloaded into the former goods yard as lifting of the line continues. Photographed 25 April 1964. *R. C. Riley*